Say No to Guilt!

Your 21-Day Plan for Accepting Your Chronic
Illness and Achieving Happiness and Inner Peace

By

Kristi Patrice Carter, JD

Say No to Guilt!

Your 21-Day Plan for Accepting Your Chronic Illness and Achieving Happiness and Inner Peace

Copyright © 2016 Kristi Patrice Carter, JD

For information, contact:

Thang Publishing Company
332 South Michigan Avenue, Suite 1032, #T610
Chicago, IL 60604-4434

http://www.successthang.com

Free VIP Readers Group Offer

Want a free report specifically for chronic illness warriors who desire unconditional love and acceptance? Kristi Patrice Carter is offering Learning to Love Myself As I Am for free (no strings attached). This amazing report is available to members of her VIP readers group. To download it, click hyperlink or visit
https://www.instafreebie.com/free/nkteb

NOTE FROM THE AUTHOR

This book is based on personal experience, interviews with other chronic illness warriors, and research conducted by the author and her freelance staff. Although much effort was made to ensure that all information in the book is factual and accurate, this book is sold with the understanding that the author assumes no responsibility for oversights, discrepancies, or inaccuracies. This book is not intended to replace medical, financial, legal, or other professional advice. Readers are reminded to use their own good judgment before applying any ideas presented in this book.

Table of Contents

Acknowledgments

This book is dedicated to:

My loving husband and best friend, Delanza Shun-tay Carter, for encouraging me to write this book, for being supportive when I experienced painful fibro flare-ups and wanted to give up, and for his innate ability to occupy the kids with various activities so I could complete this book.

My daughter, Kristin Carter, for coming up with the title of the book, assisting me with my prelaunch social media marketing efforts, and acting as a sounding board for creative ideas.

My sons, Shaun Carter and Daniel Carter, for listening to me as I read my drafts, offering me great advice, and encouraging me to "get that book done" so we could do something fun!

My mom, Christina Tarr, who has always offered unwavering love and support, helped out in every way possible to make my writing dreams a reality, and encouraged my writing efforts (from my very first story about a sick little girl named Nan who stayed home from school to the crafting of this book many years later).

My father, Lavon Tarr, for loving me and not complaining when Mom came over.

My grandmother, Fannie Lee Richardson, for her incredible strength, consistent faith, and positive attitude while going through her own medical challenge and emerging victorious.

My mother-in-law, Michelle Carter, for unselfishly making delicious meals and treats for the family; and my father-in-law, Barney Lee Carter, for picking up the kiddos; and to both of my in-laws for always being willing to help out in a pinch to accommodate my writing time.

My best friend, Angela Whitaker-Payton (Moinks); my sister, Dana B. Robinson; Aunt Barbara Rhodes; Aunt Patricia J. Ray (Patty Cake); adopted mom, Darlene Norem-Smith (Mama D); adopted grandmom, Gladys Crump; cousins Lucy Beal, Alison Turner, and Chanda Conrad-Taylor; and all my other amazing family members and friends (not mentioned here) who encouraged me to write my book and to never give up on my dream of helping others!

My researchers, idea generators, and best writing buddies, Christy Mossburg and Geradina Tomacruz; my editors, Andy Shaw and Denise Ann Barker; my graphic designer, Alex, for designing my dynamic eBook cover; and my proofreader, Amy Shelby. Without your assistance, this book would not have been possible.

Finally, and most importantly, I would like to give a heartfelt thanks to all the chronic illness warriors who are reading this book. I understand that change isn't easy and that, when you have a chronic illness, it can be downright crippling. I applaud you for your unyielding commitment to change, and I am confident that you will accomplish all your goals, in your own time.

Living with a chronic illness sucks.

Let's just get that out of the way. I know it personally, and I know you must think it once or twice or a million times a day. Anyone who says otherwise isn't being completely honest.

OK, fine. But here's the thing—**your life doesn't have to suck because you have a chronic illness.**

I know. I know. Life with a chronic illness is extremely difficult. It's so damn hard. It's frustrating. It's annoying. It's lonely. It's scary. It's draining. Some days are easier than others. Some days you feel almost normal and can accomplish so much on your to-do list, and other days you can't do anything but breathe. And here I am saying you can overcome it.

I hear you. I understand your frustration. I feel your pain. I see your struggles. I empathize with you as someone who has gone through it, hit rock bottom on the depression sector but came back with a new more positive outlook on life with a chronic illness. I also won't let you give up. I won't let you quit, as you're too close to winning.

Take it from one chronic illness warrior to another—**you absolutely can't let your illness steal your joy or rob you of happiness and inner peace.**

You can't let the guilt of being ill murder your dreams and kill your hope.

You are a warrior, and you have the power to change your story, mold it, recreate it, and make it better than before. You have the power to change your inner dialogue, rewrite your life story, and achieve greater happiness and more peace.

You may even have some doubts that you can change. You may feel uncertain or skeptical. You may have tried it all before, but nothing worked. You may have even read a ton of books on happiness, peace, and tranquility but still feel empty inside.

I know how you feel because I did that too. I have read countless books, and none had staying power simply because they weren't written by a chronic illness warrior, like you. None understood the exact challenges of someone with a chronic illness. Now that's about to change with *Say No to Guilt*.

Here's my story.

I've been fighting with chronic migraines, fibromyalgia, and chronic fatigue syndrome for many years. It feels like my entire life. Naturally I learned to pace myself and to push through the fatigue and uncertainty of my condition. I learned to accomplish my goals despite my illness. I finished college and law school, got married, had three kids, and held down several jobs, owned a freelance writing business, and I did this because I had to. My drive was too strong to quit.

I have to be honest though—I thought about quitting a lot. I got depressed and felt as if my life was over. I didn't see the light at the end of the tunnel, and I only saw darkness. When I received my fibromyalgia diagnosis (on top of my other chronic illnesses), this was a huge blow to me. There were times when I let my illness control me. There were times when I spent my days in bed with excruciating pain and fatigue, feeling as if my life were over.

At times I worried about my future when I agonized over my past or when I fought my diagnoses. At times I wanted to give up. At times I felt anger and jealousy and nothing but pain. But something deep inside kept edging me on to NOT QUIT. Something edged me on to find true happiness, inner peace, and joy. Something told me that there was a way, and I just had to find the key.

I had to alleviate that nagging guilt which kept holding me back. I had to make my life better if I wanted to make peace with my illnesses.

Something told me that I had to do some inner soul work to overcome my illnesses and NOT let them define my future or me. I had to crush those inner demons and get busy making my life better. It wasn't easy, but, with time, I made it happen. I learned to change my mind-set, and my life changed.

Now I want to share my secrets with you. I want to help you make the same mind shift. I want to help you achieve what you never deemed possible. I want to watch you succeed and bask in your gloriousness.

I want to guide you as you eliminate blame, guilt, shame, and frustration from your life. I want you to find true happiness now. Real happiness that you can hold on to.

In this guide, I will share my twenty-one-day plan for releasing guilt and achieving inner peace and happiness. It doesn't matter if you're fighting asthma, arthritis, diabetes, chronic fatigue syndrome, lupus, fibro, or any other debilitating chronic condition. I am here to help you get through it—right now.

Are you ready to take this incredible journey with me? Are you ready to crush low self-esteem and slay the guilt monster? Are you excited about shifting your mind-set to happiness and peace? Are you ready to accept your condition and change your life? I am! Let's do this thang!

Say No to Guilt!

Day 1

Why Making Peace with Your Condition Is Vital

Most chronic illness warriors with a chronic health condition often feel as if they're fighting a losing battle.

On one hand, they may have the urge to fight for better health, and, on the other hand, they likely feel the urge to surrender to their illness. Some warriors even push themselves so hard, pretending that their condition doesn't exist and hasn't affected their quality of life.

Although both methods may work for you, it's almost always best to take the middle road of accepting your medical condition and its limitations, and then fighting to improve your life. After all, your chronic illness is a part of your life, but it doesn't have to define who you are and what you can accomplish. By accepting your chronic illness and working toward improving the quality of your life, you will ultimately feel a sense of inner peace and happiness.

In contrast, when you fight your illness and resist it—by pushing yourself to the limits or simply ignoring your illness—you ultimately set yourself up for failure and defeat.

Which of the two situations below sound more like you?

Maggie has chronic fatigue syndrome and works full time as an attorney for a prestigious law firm. She was diagnosed with chronic fatigue syndrome last year, and she refuses to change her work schedule. Instead of taking on fewer cases, she has volunteered for more cases. Since she is one of the only female associates at the firm, she feels as if she has to push and work harder than others to gain the respect and admiration of her colleagues.

Maggie works fifty hours a week or more, and she rarely has time for herself or her family. In fact, when she comes home from work, she is exhausted, tired, and frustrated. She goes right to bed and doesn't wake up until the next day. Although she loves her husband and three-year-old daughter very much, she rarely spends any time with them. As a result, she feels guilty, stressed, significant emotional pain, and fatigued, even after sleeping all night. Maggie has no quality of life, and she is not happy.

Becky has chronic fatigue syndrome and is an attorney also. She too works for a prestigious law firm, but she has negotiated for a part-to-full-time position. Her caseload is significantly less than Maggie's, and Becky enjoys her work tremendously. When hired, Becky let everyone know about her condition and the fact that she would not be able to work excessive hours. She is allowed to telecommute up to three times a week, and typically rests and paces herself throughout the day. After work, Becky feels exhilarated and enjoys spending quality time with her husband and child. Her marriage is strong, and she feels happy, stress-free, and proud that she is working with her illness instead of working against it.

The difference between Maggie and Becky is astounding. Maggie has not yet accepted her limitations, and pushes herself to the limit and then some. Her symptoms are severe, and she is unhappy and experiences inner turmoil. Becky, on the other hand, has made peace with her chronic condition. She works reduced and flexible hours for a firm that understands and respects her limitations. Ultimately Becky feels happier and more at peace.

You may be wondering how you can get to this feeling of acceptance. In most instances, you have to go through the five stages of grief, and then commit to accepting your medical condition and working through it.

Stage One: Denial

The first stage toward acceptance is denial and it is extremely common in chronic illness warriors. In this stage, we attempt to deny that we're ill or that we've gone through some life-altering situation. Denial makes you think things, like the doctors made a mistake (oh, how I wish they did too), or you're a good person so God wouldn't let you have a chronic condition (God still loves you unconditionally, and a chronic illness can happen to anyone unfortunately), etc.

While denial is a normal part of the grieving process, remaining too long in this (or any of the stages of grief) can prove to be detrimental to our happiness. Too often people remain in the denial stage of their illness and push too hard, worsening their situation. There is nothing wrong with challenging ourselves to be better, yet we can't pretend like our lives haven't changed. We can't bury our heads in the sand and push past our breaking points. We can't refuse to seek out traditional or holistic treatments that might help because we refuse to believe that we're dealing with a medical condition.

Although it's great to have hope and faith, we can't deny the problem exists. Yes, we may question life, in general, and wonder why we're living our current life with this chronic condition. We may feel utter disbelief and shock. We may, at times, question our lives and how we can go on, but we can't deny that a chronic illness exists. Instead we must recognize denial as the initial part of the grieving process.

Stage Two: Anger

Anger comes after we move past denial and realize that we do have a chronic illness and that there is a real possibility we will have this illness for a very long time. Some people get angry with their bodies, or God, or another higher power. They even get angry with family members, whom they love dearly. In essence, they get mad that this illness has crept into and changed their lives. This anger is often coupled with immense guilt that we have badly treated those we love, and this guilt then makes us angrier. It's a terrible and vicious cycle.

When you're feeling angry, understand that this is also part of the healing process. Allow yourself to feel mad and irate. Although you shouldn't take out your feeling on others, you should still understand that you have a right to feel the way you do. You may feel abandoned, alone, and deserted. You may feel as if God or your higher power doesn't care about you. Those who use anger to uncover their fears and deal with them will move on to the next phases quickly.

Stage Three: Bargaining

The third stage is called bargaining, but, when it comes to chronic illness warriors, this might very well be called *rebounding*. In this stage, we attempt to do something about our illness. We may bargain with our higher power to take away our chronic illness, even knowing it doesn't really work like that. We may promise to spend more time volunteering or doing something nice for someone else. We may bargain with God to take away our illness so that we can be healthy again: "God, if You could just do this one thing for me, I promise I'll never miss church again." Sound familiar? We may be filled with "*what if*s" or "*if only*" statements. But we need to realize what's happened has happened, and no amount of bargaining will fix that.

Stage Four: Depression

Many warriors who have gone through the bargaining process next go through a period of depression. In this stage, we are typically very focused on the present. We feel alone, down, and frustrated. We may feel a deep sense of loss and sadness that goes to the very core of who we are. Many refer to this stage as *preparatory grieving*, which is quite necessary for acceptance. If you feel depressed, don't be down on yourself. To feel regret, uncertainty, and grief is completely normal. These feelings demonstrate that you are human and that acceptance is getting closer. In most instances, you may feel as if your depressed feelings will never end.

However, the depression will certainly end and is typically experienced because you have lost your life as you know it. In many instances, people withdraw from others during this period and may isolate themselves. They may even question the purpose of their life—other than simply having this chronic pain and illness. It's crucial in this stage not to push away those who are trying to be there for you, even if it's just letting them know you need some space rather than ignoring them completely.

Stage Five: Acceptance

Acceptance is often confused with the notion of being "all right" or "OK" with what is happening. This is not the case. We will never like this reality or agree that it is OK, but eventually we accept it. We learn to live with it. Our conditions become the new norm with which we must learn to live. Acceptance is the last stage of grief. Like anything else, it takes a great deal of time to get here.

Acceptance is the point at which you say to yourself, "OK, maybe the things I now experience are real. Maybe I am not well. After all, there's no basis in reality for any of my beliefs that I am whole and healed, and I've noticed that—when I take my meds or holistic remedies—I seem to feel better. Maybe there's something to this chronic illness."

To accept things, to move on, and to get better though, you need an inner intuition to realize you're sick. You need fear to motivate you to conquer it. Most of all you need hope that one day things will get better. This final phase is marked by a physical withdrawal and a mental calm. This is not a period of happiness and yet must be distinguished from depression. Finding acceptance may be just having more good days than bad ones. Reaching acceptance opens up your mind to the memories you may have blocked because they were too painful. You can focus on what matters the most and move forward with your life.

What can you do to set yourself up for success?

Before we dive into my plan for you, I'd like you to take some time right now to think about whether you've gone through or are currently in a specific stage of grief.

How did you get through the process? What coping mechanisms did you use? Have you truly accepted your chronic condition? If not, why not? Have you made any modifications to your life so that you can accept your condition? If so, what modifications have you made? If not, what modifications can you make?

Notes:

_____
_____
_____
_____
_____
_____
_____

Next, I want you to commit to giving yourself time to go through the grieving process but that you won't get stuck in any one stage. Repeat after me:

"I understand that I have a chronic illness, and, although I won't let it define me, I will work with it to improve the quality of my life. I will accept my limitations, and I will not fight against my condition. I will not put unnecessary stress on myself. I will not be angry at myself or others. I will work with my body so that I can increase my inner peace and happiness. I will start today."

Day 2

Unconditional Love for Yourself

Recap:

Yesterday we discussed the importance of making peace with your condition. We talked about the five stages of grief including denial, anger, bargaining, depression, and acceptance. We committed to not fight with our condition. Now we must display unconditional love to ourselves.

You are amazing, fantastic, remarkable, outstanding, and incredibly special. You have a unique and divine purpose. You matter. You matter a whole lot.

Reread that paragraph. Let it soak in. Everything else I have to say won't matter if you can't start accepting these truths about yourself.

Even if you've spent the majority of your past disliking or even hating yourself, annoyed by your condition and betrayed by your body, you can now switch off the inner hate button and turn on the self-love trigger.

You no longer have to feel self-hatred or loathing. You no longer have to feel sadness, shame, and low self-esteem whenever you experience a flare-up or can't do something because you're not well.

You no longer have to spend your days feeling unhappy, discontent, and secretly hating people who are healthier than you. You can let go of hopelessness, insecurity, and shame for being—wait for it—not well.

Yes, you aren't well, but your condition is not your fault. You didn't do something to bring on your illness, and you must stop hating yourself for not being better physically right now.

Trust me. Your body wants nothing more than to function properly. It isn't trying to harm you. It desperately wants to achieve health too. It wants to feel better, and it wants you to feel better as well.

So push aside these negative and defeating feelings, and replace them with an abundance of PURE UNCONDITIONAL and UNADULTERATED LOVE.

What's holding you back? I have an inkling: you feel that, since you are your illness and you hate your illness, you, therefore, hate yourself. Sounds about right, doesn't it?

No. It's not right. **You may have an illness, but you are not your illness**. You don't have to allow your condition to control or alter the loving person you are at your core.

By learning to love yourself, your outlook and your life will improve drastically.

Contrary to what you may think, this is not some mumbo-jumbo hippie stuff. It isn't. Loving yourself is the single most important thing you must do to find inner peace and happiness.

Every day you must be willing to love yourself deeply, despite your condition, in spite of any pain or bothersome symptoms. You must be willing to love yourself now. Not after your medical team finds a cure. Not after you get better chronic pain management. Not after you find a spouse, lose ten pounds, or whatever other conditions and milestones you have labeled as the criteria for when you can love yourself. Those beliefs are just acting as artificial barriers.

You have to love yourself right now—today!

So today's assignment is for you to realize self-love is buried deep inside you.

Even if you don't know it yet, you do love yourself; and your body, mind, and spirit love you right back. Still not convinced? Consider this. Every freaking day, your body works hard for you to get you through those tough days. Your heart pumps blood through your body; your lungs circulate air; your spirit aches for something more out of your life than lying around and feeling sorry for yourself. Ultimately your body, mind, and spirit do all this even though you tell your body how much you hate and despise it.

Let me explain something. It's perfectly normal for you to feel frustrated and angry about your illness. It's OK for you to feel sad, even depressed, because you can't do all the things you used to do or want to do. I get it. I've been there too.

But you know what?

- It's not OK for you to hate yourself day in and day out.

- It's not OK for you to abuse your body with unhealthy foods or tell your body how much you hate it every chance you get.

- It's not OK for you to wake up and only see your body with pure disgust, complete with major flaws and imperfections.

These negative feelings are simply not OK.

Example time. Let's consider these two young ladies. Shauna has rheumatoid arthritis and has had it for ten years. She can no longer do the things she used to do, but she truly loves herself. Every morning she looks in the mirror and smiles about her life. She recognizes that she is ten pounds overweight, but she doesn't allow the extra pounds to define her. She knows that her body is fighting a hard fight every day.

Shauna feels comforted because she is doing the best she can under her current situation. She takes her medication and holistic remedies every day; she exercises when she can, and she accepts her condition for what it is. Shauna has learned to work with her pain levels by alleviating stress and not pushing herself past her limits.

Shauna easily looks in the mirror and says, "Hey, beautiful. You're looking good today. I love you, Shauna. Today is a new day, and I am incredibly proud of you for all your accomplishments." Whenever Shauna feels negativity and doubt creeping in, she flips the switch to see the good in the situation.

In contrast, Shauna's sister, Meghan, who also has rheumatoid arthritis, hates her life, despises her body, and fights her illness on a daily basis. She berates herself every chance she gets. Meghan can't look in the mirror without telling herself how ugly, disgusting, and awful she is. She feels guilt when she can't exercise or hang out with her friends. She is not open to traditional or holistic medications because she believes that nothing will help her. Meghan stays in bed and watches her life pass, like a slow and depressing movie. She complains about her pain every minute of every day and has allowed her deep sense of self-loathing to lead her down a negative path.

After hearing about Shauna and Meghan, which chronic illness warrior can you best relate to? To be honest, I used to be like Meghan, and then I decided to become more like Shauna. The change happened when I decided to lead a life of fulfillment, peace, and happiness. Like Shauna, I made a commitment and changed my life. You can too!

Today's Activities:

Today, start seeing yourself as the remarkable and phenomenal person you are. You'll reprogram your mind to be your best friend and supporter. You'll dismiss negativity and instill higher self-control within you. You'll recognizing your goodness and build yourself up instead of pulling yourself down.

1. Commit to loving yourself right now despite your illness. Repeat after me:

"I am committed to loving myself right now. I am not perfect, but I am fantastic. I am a dynamic human being, and my life has purpose and meaning. I will love myself despite any imperfections. Those imperfections make me—me. I am grateful for everything my body does on a daily basis to keep me alive and uplifted. My body and I are working toward better health, and I will love myself unconditionally— starting today!"

2. Five minutes of loving-yourself mirror work. Look in the mirror for at least five minutes and tell yourself that you're valuable, important, and loved. Look deep into your eyes and say, "I'm a warrior. I am [insert your name], and I love myself very much." Repeat this for at least two minutes. If you're not comfortable expressing love for yourself or talking to yourself in a mirror, that's fine. Simply tell yourself, "Hi, [insert your name]. I'm willing to love you." Rinse and repeat.

3. Find at least five positive characteristics that describe you. Make sure they represent how you see yourself or how you want to see yourself in the near future. Reflect on these qualities and allow the pride to overcome you and then write them down.

1. I am _____.

2. I am _____.

3. I am _____.

4. I am _____.

5. I am _____.

Once you've written them down, read them over and over throughout the course of the day. Repeat them at least three times out loud to let the messages sink deep into your subconscious mind.

4. Be your best friend and supporter. Understand that you are fighting a hard battle and that you are in control of your life and your experiences. Write down five things you can do today to help you feel better about your medical condition. List five activities that you can do today that will bring you inner peace and joy. They don't necessarily have to be big things. Simple things work as well.

Examples: meditation, yoga, massage, reading a good book, taking a warm bath, etc.

    1. _____

    2. _____

    3. _____

    4. _____

    5. _____

5. Treat yourself. Set aside thirty minutes to do something really special for yourself. Preferably I'd like you to do all five things listed in #4 above. But, if that is not realistic, at least do one thing. The point is that you must do something to show yourself that you are loved and appreciated and that you plan on putting your needs first and rewarding yourself for being the incredible person you are!

Notes:

_____
_____
_____
_____
_____
_____

Day 3

Defining Happiness

Recap

The last couple days we talked about making peace with ourselves and accepting our conditions for what they are. We completed a few exercises and made a commitment to our happiness. Yesterday we focused on loving ourselves unconditionally. We acknowledged that we are special, unique, and highly favored. We engaged in a bit of mirror work and gave ourselves permission to feel proud of our accomplishments (no matter how big or small) and those unique characteristics that make us—us. We spent time doing at least one activity that made us feel special, loved, and important.

Today we will focus on happiness.

Now it may seem impossible to be happy when you're chronically ill. However, happiness is possible. Some chronic illness warriors live in a state of happiness while others live in a state of depression. I've been on both ends of the spectrum, and I'll choose happiness every time.

I've lived extremely sorrowful days and jubilant happy ones. Some days I've felt as if my illness has robbed me of my life and stolen my joy. I've also felt like throwing in the towel and giving up. **But I also know how it feels to restructure your mind, choose happiness, and take back your power!**

The truth is that you are human (with superhero warrior powers of course), and it's normal for you to feel a range of emotions (especially sad ones). However, you can choose to be more happy than miserable. You can choose to experience pure unadulterated joy. You can choose to find peace and contentment with your life today. You can choose happiness in this moment—right now.

You may not be able to change your diagnosis, but you can change how you perceive your illness. You can experience more peace, love, and gratitude than you experience hate, jealousy, and pity. You can choose how to feel happier every day.

And the secret is to realize that happiness is a choice, a state where your life meets your needs (whatever those needs may be).

By choosing to restructure your life in a way that meets your needs, you too can experience more happiness every day.

Yes, it will be challenging, but you're up to the challenge. You are strong. You are a warrior, and you can do anything!

Here are a few activities to jump-start your happiness quest:

1. Write an awe narrative. Think back to a time when you felt a sense of awe regarding something you witnessed or experienced. People may experience awe when they see their newborn babies sleeping, when in the presence of a beautiful natural landscape or work of art, or when they watch a moving speech or performance. It doesn't matter what comes to mind but simply think about a situation that moves you.

Focus on that experience and truly feel the joy. Feel the sense of awe. Once you identify something, describe it in writing with as much detail as possible. Try doing this for fifteen minutes each and every day. Research suggests that awe involves sensing the presence of something greater than one's self, along with decreased self-consciousness and a decreased focus on minor everyday concerns. Experiences of awe have been shown to improve life satisfaction.

2. Keep a gratitude journal. Studies have traced a range of impressive benefits to the simple act of writing down the things for which we're grateful—benefits including better sleep, fewer symptoms of illness, and more happiness. In many of the studies, people were simply instructed to record five things they experienced in the past week for which they're grateful. The entries are supposed to be brief—just a single sentence.

This weekly practice is about forcing ourselves to pay attention to the good things in life which we'd otherwise take for granted. You don't need to buy a fancy personal journal, or worry about spelling or grammar. The important thing is to establish the habit of paying attention to gratitude-inspiring events.

3. *It's a Wonderful Life* yourself. For fifteen minutes each day, take a moment to think about a positive event in your life, such as an educational or career achievement, the birth of a child, or a special trip you took. Think back to the time of this event and the circumstances that made it possible. Consider the ways in which this event might never have happened.

Write down all the possible situations and decisions—large and small—that could have gone differently and prevented this event from occurring. **Imagine what your life would be like now if you hadn't enjoyed this positive event and all the fruits that flowed from it.** Shift your focus to remind yourself that this event actually did happen and reflect upon the benefits it brought you. Now that you have considered how things might have turned out differently, appreciate that these benefits were not inevitable in your life. Allow yourself to feel grateful that things happened as they did.

Today's Activity:

If you find yourself having trouble keeping positive thoughts, try looking in the mirror and **repeating this affirmation**:

"I will not allow my chronic illness to prevent me from pursuing all the happiness life has to offer."

It matters not which exercise you choose to do today. Just do something to improve the quality of your life.

Do something that will ultimately **help you refocus your energies** on seeing that **your life has purpose and meaning**.

Do this and you'll soon see that your time is best spent being grateful for the experiences and people you *do* have rather than lamenting what you don't have; you'll be well on your way then.

Day 4

Creating a Vision Board for Happiness

Recap

On Day 1, we talked about making peace with ourselves and accepting our conditions for what they are. We completed a few exercises and made a commitment to our happiness. On Day 2, we focused on loving ourselves unconditionally. We acknowledged that we are special, unique, and highly favored. We engaged in a bit of mirror work and gave ourselves permission to feel proud of our accomplishments (no matter how big or small) and those unique characteristics that make us, us. We spent time doing at least one activity that made us feel special, loved, and important. Then on Day 3, we sought more happiness, remembering a feeling of awe and keeping a gratitude journal.

To help you on your quest, we're going to now focus on creating our very own happiness vision board.

Many of us start the New Year by making resolutions, and then, by the end of January, we've forgotten what we resolved to change in our lives. Want proof of that? Just count the number of people in a gym on January 2 compared to January 30.

Whether you are making intentions, resolutions, or goals, it can be hard to stick to them. After all, life happens, and those dreams fall by the wayside.

To prevent this from occurring in your life and to ensure that happiness remains your number one priority, you must have an overall vision for happiness in your mind. When you do so, you can pull from this memory when things get tough. You can visualize your happier, more contented self when you're filled with doubt and negativity. It's like breaking the emergency glass to pull the fire alarm when you question whether you can be happy—and a flood of happy thoughts will douse the doubt fire.

You can see yourself being joyful in the present moment. You can remind your ego self that nothing—not even you—can get in the way of your own happiness. Through visualization and specifically a vision board, we are less likely to retreat into bitter complaints, worry, and stress, ultimately leading us to live a life of peace and freedom.

Now what exactly is a happiness vision board? **Vision boards are tools that display pictures and affirmations of the goals and things you desire in life**. They help you focus your energy on your specific goals and attract that same energy back to you.

They require your senses—thinking about your goals, seeing the pictures that engage your subconscious mind to go after them, and reminding you of actions to take to accomplish those goals. A happiness vision board focuses on those things that make you happy, on those things that generate feelings of contentment when you look at them.

Here are some tips to help you create your vision board for happiness:

1. Choose your happiness goals. Think about your goals for a happier life. What do you want your life to look like one year from now or five or ten? What top ten things make you happy? Your vision board can be about one area of life or all of them. It can represent one goal or many goals that make you happy and content. Decide what you want in one or several domains of life:

- Health

- Career

- Relationship or marriage

- Family

- Friends

- Interests, hobbies, fun

- Spiritual life

- Learning and personal growth

- Financial

- Service

2. Collect pictures and words. After you have chosen your goals, cut out pictures from magazines or online printouts that represent the specific goals you want to accomplish. Include items that lift your spirit and excite you. You can also find sites online that will help you create a virtual vision board.

Look for the kind of house you want, with the right kind of yard for you. Include a picture of the book you plan to write; add a picture of your happy family having summer vacation fun. Be sure to include a picture or photo of yourself in the collage. Paste your pictures and words on poster paper, construction paper, display boards, presentation boards, or something you might frame.

3. Display your vision board to view it daily. Put your happiness vision board in a prominent place so you will see it every day. Look at it for about five minutes at least twice a day. Think about the beautiful scenes representing your goals and how you feel when you look at them. See yourself living your goals and feeling the happy emotions as your dreams come to life. Feel yourself with the top down in your new convertible. Feel the joy of writing a check to your favorite charity. Feel the excitement when boarding the cruise ship. Experience the living results of your goals and stay positive.

It can be helpful to display affirmations prominently on your vision board. Here's an **affirmation** you could use for this purpose:

"I am worthy of all the best life has to offer."

If that one doesn't strike your fancy, the Internet is full of hundreds of positive affirmations you can use. Creating a vision board for happiness is a fun and creative way to attract to you what you want in life and to improve your overall outlook.

Today's Activity:

Create a happiness vision board right now. Don't delay. Get busy and fill it with your desires. Make it personalized and special so that you are encouraged whenever you look at it.

Day 5

Recognizing Thoughts and Why They Matter

Recap

The last few days, we made peace with ourselves and accepted our conditions for what they are. We made a commitment to our happiness. We focused on loving ourselves unconditionally, acknowledging that we are special, loved, unique, and highly favored while doing at least one activity daily that made us feel important. Then we started a gratitude journal and created our very own happiness vision board, focusing on the importance of pure unbridled happiness, what happiness is, and how to increase your levels of happiness.

Today we will focus on our thoughts and how they can derail our efforts to be happier.

Let's Dive Right In

Today we will build upon the foundation of unconditional love but take it a step further. We will pay close attention to the thousands of thoughts we have on a daily basis. Without judgment, we will notice whether those thoughts encourage, motivate, inspire, or cause us anxiety, fear, or sadness.

Although we will eventually learn to transform our thoughts into more positive ones, today we will focus on recognizing our thought patterns without judgment. We will simply practice being aware of our thoughts by recognizing and writing them down.

Thoughts are the windows to our soul, and they are the vehicle by which we travel toward inner peace and happiness.

So, by learning to recognize our recurring thought patterns, we can ultimately improve our levels of happiness and the quality of our lives.

Let's delve into the science of thoughts, types of thoughts, and how they help us create the life we want to lead. According to the Merriam-Webster dictionary, thoughts are the action of thinking; it is cognition. It is the process of thinking and creating.

Psychology Today estimates that we have between 25,000–50,000 thoughts every single day.

Even more amazing, of these thousands of thoughts, around 70% are estimated to be negative.

Whoa! That means that the majority of us chronic illness warriors are not only dealing with our illness but we're walking around with a whopping 70% of our thoughts being negative. Thoughts that are ultimately invading our heads and making our situations appear worse.

Even crazier (and, yes, it gets worse), most of us probably don't even realize that we have these thoughts flooding our brains. To make it even harder to figure out, we have both conscious and unconscious thoughts every day.

Our conscious mind processes logical thoughts, reasoning abilities, and our intentional actions. Our unconscious mind is the primary source of human behavior; it holds feelings and judgments. It holds things we see and think about but not necessarily intentionally.

And then there is the subconscious mind. Right in between conscious and unconscious, it holds beliefs, values, and motivations.

With so many thoughts each day and so many negative ones circling around, how important are the thoughts we have? Answer: extremely important!

Thoughts are all the things that our brains process and create. If most of our thoughts are negative, then our views on life are most likely negative too. Daily thoughts can come from our conscious and our subconscious mind. But the subconscious mind is where most thoughts gain entrance into the conscious mind.

By having a better understanding of this phenomenon, we can become more aware of our thoughts so that we can ultimately get better control of our lives.

Let's consider the Law of Attraction, where you ultimately attract into your life what you focus on. If you focus on bad things and allow negative thoughts to rule your life constantly, then those negative things will appear in your life even more. It matters not if these thoughts are conscious or unconscious.

Don't follow me? Consider this: Ever notice how a bad day can start with something simple and minor, like spilling coffee on your clothes, or waking up late? From the moment the one bad thing happens, our day seems to get worse and worse, especially if we focus on what an awful, horrible day we're having.

The key is to change this negative thought process into one that is more positive and uplifting.

Now think of the same scenario but, instead of replaying the incident over and over, we look at the brighter side. We tell ourselves, *well, at least I have another shirt to wear, or I got an extra bit of rest that I needed.* By choosing to be more positive, we can change the outlook of our entire day. We can take a negative experience and make it more positive. So we can bring more of what is good into our lives and less of what isn't.

Hopefully now you realize that the power of thoughts is extremely important for changing our lives for the better. By spending some time writing down our thoughts, we can get a better feel for our thought patterns. Remember, however, that we must do this without judgment.

Today's Activity:

Sit down with a timer set for five to ten minutes. During this time, you should let your thoughts wander. Just let them flow. After the timer goes off, write down any thoughts you had and what (if anything) triggered the thought. Then put away the list.

The point of this exercise is to demonstrate that we have thousands of thoughts a day, and these very thoughts ultimately control our world. By recognizing the nature of our thoughts, we can ultimately change them for the better. However, we first have to be aware of them.

Actual Thoughts	Trigger for Thoughts (if any)

Notes:

_____

_____

_____

_____

_____

_____

_____

_____

_____

_____

_____

Say No to Guilt!

Day 6

Turning Negative Thoughts into Positive Ones

Recap

So far, (1) We made peace with ourselves and our conditions, committing to our happiness. (2) We focused on self-love expressed by doing at least one activity daily that made us feel important. (3) We started a gratitude journal. (4) Created our very own happiness vision board to increase our levels of happiness.

Yesterday we evaluated the difference between conscious, subconscious, and subconscious thoughts. We spent time letting our minds run free and evaluating our thoughts (without judgment). We wrote down our thoughts. Were you surprised by what you wrote down?

Let's Dive In

Today we will evaluate our thoughts a bit further. We will not only write down more of our thoughts but we'll determine whether these are positive or negative. We will figure out how many of our thoughts are negative, any triggers for them, how those thoughts made us feel, and how we could turn them into positive thoughts.

We will evaluate how our thoughts correlate to how we feel about our illness, our happiness levels, our lives, and ourselves.

As the saying goes: *change your thoughts, change your world.*

When we have a better grip on our thoughts, we can have a more positive effect in our lives. It's just that simple.

Positive thinking can make pain levels go down. Remarkable, isn't it? Don't believe me? I'm a prime example.

I've been in excruciating pain due to a fibromyalgia flare-up. I've felt weak and worn out. As you might imagine, this pain quickly turned my conscious and subconscious thoughts into only negative ones. But the effects of positive thinking turned things around for me.

Reframing my negativity when dealing with chronic pain not only helped me reduce pain levels but also helped to control the speed, the frequency, and the intensity of my fibromyalgia flare-ups. It also led to an increase in my overall happiness in a very short period. It's true, and the same can happen to you!

Need more convincing? Consider this example.

Let's say that you have a negative thought from your subconscious mind regarding chronic pain. Someone says something to you about your chronic pain targeting weak-minded people, who aren't strong enough to manage their conditions.

Your subconscious mind, which holds your beliefs and values, then forms the thought, *I am weak*, or *I don't deserve a normal life*, or *This is just how my life is now. I can't control it.*

In reality this situation isn't out of control; your thoughts are.

- You **haven't done anything to deserve** this chronic pain.

- You **aren't weak because you have a chronic illness**.

- You aren't weak because **someone thinks you're weak**.

Instead you have the **power to change your life** and how you perceive your chronic illness and pain levels.

In the above example, your subconscious mind will only be filled with overwhelmingly negative thought patterns if you allow them to be there. These constant negative thoughts can increase your pain levels without you even being aware of it.

For example, all-over body tenseness and muscle alertness means you're not allowing your body to relax. This stressor can happen because of negative subconscious thoughts. Your body may believe that you aren't safe or secure because of these thoughts.

In a 2005 study at Wake Forest Baptist Medical Center, researchers **found a 28% pain rating decrease** when patients expected less pain from an impending medical event. In other studies, researchers have consistently found a link between positive thoughts and higher immunity levels. Mayo Clinic studies have shown how being more optimistic can positively affect physical health by reducing the stress levels in your body.

Once you stop your negative thoughts as they creep into your mind and replace them with a positive thought, your stress level decreases.

What you need to do now.

Now that you know what negative thoughts can do and want to learn how to replace them with positive ones, what techniques can you use to achieve this?

1. Just like yesterday, I want you to set your timer for five to ten minutes, and then sit down and let your thoughts run wild. Write down your thoughts and any triggers, how a thought made you feel, how you responded, and what emotions you felt

during this time. This exercise is a little more detailed than yesterday's exercise, but it can help you better identify stressful situations in which negative thoughts can affect your body and its pain levels.

2. Take a look at these thoughts. Were they more negative or positive or a combination of both?

3. Practice turning a negative thought into a positive one.

4. Engage in positive self-talk and use **affirmations** to replace those nagging negative thoughts. For instance, if your thought was, *"I'll never get better,"* change it to *"I'm getting better every single day."* Change *"My body is so sick"* to *"My body is working hard to improve its health."* Change *"I'm depressed"* to *"I'm learning how to feel happier each moment."*

When you recognize a negative thought pattern, say something else, like, *"I am stronger than this,"* or *"I have the power to control my thoughts,"* or *"My pain is a liar. I can handle this."*

Today's Activity:

Sit down and take a few minutes to define your triggers.

Actual Thoughts Trigger My Feelings and My Responses

Write Down Your Thoughts (both positive and negative)	Triggers	How Did You Feel? (Include your emotions as well as your body's sensations)	How Did You Respond? (Include your emotions as well as your body's sensations)

Say No to Guilt!

Day 7

Thought-Stopping Process – Reframing Your Thoughts

Recap

I hope your earlier commitment to your happiness has been expressing itself over the last six days in self-love, keeping a gratitude journal, visiting your happiness vision board twice a day, and evaluating your thoughts (without judgment). Plus you have already practiced seeing the difference between negative or positive thoughts; you are aware of any triggers, and you have worked on changing negative thoughts into positive ones.

That's so much progress! Think of how you approach the day now that you can harness those skills. But let's take this concept a bit further. There's value in doing a deeper dive in this crucial area. When I first realized that 90% of my thoughts were negative, I was flabbergasted.

The good news is that I immediately used this information as feedback and made a conscious decision to focus on positive thinking!

Why Chronic Illness Warriors Benefit the Most

This strategy is especially important for chronic illness warriors, like you and me.

- We often feel extremely down on ourselves because we feel stuck with our condition.

- We feel as if little or anything we do can manifest happiness.

- We feel like there isn't a silver lining out there for us.

Did any of the above sound familiar? The good news is that these are fallacies. We are more in control of our lives than we might think. By changing our thoughts, we ultimately change our world.

By learning how to switch from negative to positive thoughts, we, in essence, will feel more happiness, inner peace, and tranquility.

You'll be increasingly likely to feel more energized—despite the limitations your condition has placed on you—if you take control of your thoughts instead of letting your thoughts control you. Tried it once and it didn't work? This truly is a "practice makes perfect" thing; the more you practice this technique, the better you'll get at it.

By learning to cancel those negative thoughts and to replace them with positive ones, you can and will take back your power, and demonstrate your confidence and inner strength. By mastering this strategy, you will be well on your way to a better life.

So today let's make it happen. Let's spend this day crushing those negative thoughts whenever they come out. Let's practice stopping them—canceling them out and doing what's needed to turn them around.

Here are some strategies you can use today to crush negative thinking. Since this is very personal, feel free to use these strategies as you wish, to recreate them to your liking, or simply to mix and match. It's most important to find a strategy that works for you.

1. **Breathe deeply.** Take ten deep breaths as you count to ten. When you notice any negative thoughts clouding your mind, you must immediately refocus those thoughts. You then take the negative thoughts and transform them into positive ones. Here's an example: Let's say that the thought comes in *"I'm so sick. I will never get better."* Flip the script. Take that initial thought and say out loud, *"I am not yet well, but I am getting better every day. In time, my health will improve."* You are realistic yet optimistic. You aren't denying anything, but you're not wallowing in the negative.

2. **Mind crush those negative thoughts.** With this exercise, you imagine your negative thought as a balloon or leaf. Once you identify that negative thought, you immediately let it float away, or you pop it. You learn to let go of those negative thoughts so that you have better control over your mind and any negativity. And who doesn't want to mind crush something?

3. **Cancel. Cancel. Cancel those negative thoughts.** When a negative thought permeates your mind, recognize it and then immediately say out loud, *"Cancel. Cancel."* Then replace that negative thought with a more positive and empowering one. For instance, let's say you have a thought *"I am fat."* Immediately you say out loud, *"Cancel. Cancel. Cancel. I'm making progress toward controlling my food portions,"* or *"I'm making better food choices every day"* or something similar.

4. **Hum, hum, hum away those negative thoughts.** Another fun technique is to play a humming game. With this strategy you hum a favorite song like "Row, Row, Row Your Boat," as soon as a negative thought pops into your brain. The chosen song should be one that makes you smile and feel happy. For me, the song "Happy" by Pharrell Williams is tremendously therapeutic. Whenever I use it to divert a negative thought, I immediately feel, well, happy!

5. **Go positivity shopping in your mind.** Visualize yourself in a grocery store full of positive "food for your soul" items. As you shop, take those negative thoughts and throw them in the trash. Simultaneously place healthier, more positive thoughts

into your cart (your mind). By filling your cart with more positive thoughts, your mood will magically shift to one of power and control. Typically a few minutes completing this exercise works spectacularly. Don't worry if you have to do this frequently throughout your day. This shopping exercise will help you retrain your brain to always find more positive, empowering thoughts.

6. **Physically get rid of negative thoughts**. It may sound a little strange, but it really can help to do something physically to these negative thoughts. When any negative thought bombards your mind, write it down on a piece of paper but take it a step further. Throw away the paper, burn it, or simply shred it. The key is to get rid of this thought (physically and mentally) as fast as you can. In 2012, Ohio State University conducted a study, and researchers found that those who wrote down a negative thought and then proceeded to get physically rid of it felt much happier and had more positive thoughts afterward. Sometimes you need to actually do something with these thoughts to get rid of them. Sports teams sometimes do this by burning jerseys from their losing season. You don't have to burn anything! Unless you want to. Whatever works.

7. **Drink milk or tea to drift those thoughts away**. Negative thoughts come from many different places and for many different reasons. Sometimes a negative thought many come from a place of loneliness and unhappiness. In 2012, Yale researchers discovered that physically warming up can give you emotional and mental comfort. So, if you are having a surge of negative thoughts, and you think some of them may be coming from a place of loneliness, grab a warm cup of soothing milk, decaffeinated tea, or coffee. With every sip, imagine you are filling up with positive thoughts instead of negative ones. Not only will this method brighten your day but it will help you quash those negative thoughts quickly and effortlessly.

8. **Reframe those thoughts with a fun activity.** With this technique, you reframe your thoughts by doing something fun. Here's how it works: The next time you have a negative thought, you simply stop focusing on that thought and switch

gears. You do something fun, like play a game. You can grab a crossword or Sudoku puzzle or play a video game to help distract you from your negative thoughts. Often this will divert your attention away from those negative thoughts and help you reframe it in a fun way.

So, as you can see, you ultimately have the power to change those negative thoughts. You have the power to change your thoughts and to change your world, and the absolute best way to do this is to use a strategy that enables you to change your thought process.

Today's Activity:

Choose one of the eight suggestions listed above for crushing your negative thoughts. Feel free to try others. Find your favorites and use them daily.

Notes:

_____
_____
_____
_____
_____
_____
_____
_____
_____
_____
_____

Say No to Guilt!

Day 8

Be Grateful

Recap

Over the first four days we committed to our happiness goal by expressing self-love, keeping a gratitude journal, visiting our happiness vision board twice daily, and evaluating our thoughts (without judgment).

For the last three days we focused on the power of positive thinking. We tracked our thoughts, how they made us feel, noticed any triggers for negativity, and focused on replacing negative thoughts with positive ones. We learned how to take control of our thoughts so we could empower and change our lives.

Using Gratefulness as a Foundation for Success

Today we will continue with more positive thinking, and we'll focus on being more grateful for the many blessings that we experience on a daily basis.

"Grateful?" you might ask with heavy sarcasm. "How can I be grateful when I'm ill and in pain?"

I understand that you may not feel like being grateful. In fact, you may feel downright ungrateful because of how different your life is with a chronic illness. These feelings are OK. I know, and I understand.

The key here is to understand that, although you might not be able to change your condition, you can change how you think about it. You can learn to be grateful right now!

Time and time again, chronic illness warriors will say, "I will be grateful when I feel better. I'll be grateful when they find a cure," etc. Although it is wonderful to have hope, it's also important to *not let your current medical condition dictate how much happiness and peace you have right now.*

The key to a guilt-free, peaceful, and happy life is to be grateful right now.

I know. I know. I'm asking a lot. But I wouldn't ask you to do anything that I couldn't do as well. In fact, while writing the last couple chapters, I had a painful fibromyalgia flare-up. The irony, right? I was being asked to practice what I preach.

That flare-up had me in bed for three days. During this time frame, it hurt to move. It hurt to write. It hurt to rest, but, most of all, it just plain hurt everywhere.

Rather than wallowing about how much pain I was in, I instead focused on all the things I had to be grateful for. I used the Jedi mind trick of refocusing negativity when thoughts came into my mind of this nature: *I'll hurt forever. I'll never get better.*

I focused on being grateful for the small blessings in my life. For instance, I focused on various comfort measures I could do right then to make myself feel better. I focused on being grateful for my heating pad, my ability to massage sore muscles and joints. I felt grateful for Icy Hot pain relieving gel, Deep Blue Rub, MSM joint/muscle pain relief cream, etc. I expressed gratitude to my wonderful husband who went out and bought me a stress ball to squeeze to help alleviate my hand pain. I felt grateful for my comfy bed and my wonderful kids, who routinely checked on me to make sure I was still alive because I was in the bed for such a very long time.

The point is, I didn't focus on the pain. I didn't think of the days I wasn't able to do the things I wanted to do. And not because it didn't really hurt that bad—because it did hurt a lot—but I chose to focus on all the blessings in my life and not all the things going wrong at that particular time.

Was it easy? No. It was freaking hard, buddy. But I'm a gal who loves a good challenge, and being grateful helped me change my outlook on my situation. It made a hopeless situation seem better. Gratitude helped me feel better and more at peace. It turned my pain-focused thoughts into a bearable physical condition and then into a positive one.

So today I'd like you to focus on gratitude too. Take a few moments to think about three things that you are grateful for right now. Don't hesitate. Let those ideas flow. Even if you don't feel grateful, I still want you to think of three things for which you're grateful. Although this may NOT feel like the natural thing to do, I want you to do it anyway. It's like eating green peas; you may have to push yourself to eat them, but, once you do (or swallow them, like I do), you can have dessert—a cookie (pure happiness).

Today's Activity:

Now I want you to write down these three things here.

Things I'm Grateful For:

1._____

2._____

3._____

You can write them here or on a piece of paper. Or you can simply get a fancy, snazzy gratitude journal to keep your notes there. The point is that I want you to write down these three things and review them at least three times today (or tomorrow for you warriors who are finishing this chapter at night).

You'll soon find that, when you write down those three things which you are grateful for, you immediately refocus your mind on things that are more positive. You feel more at peace, and you see more miracles in your life. In truth, your life just seems better.

For you technology fans who prefer to use your smartphones, you can use gratitude apps. Here are some of my favorites:

Be Grateful

With this app, you can log in, write down, and track all the things in your life you are grateful for in an easy-to-use format. You'll keep a list of items to be grateful for, which will create stats and scores to see what makes you happy. This app is easy to share and post online for anyone to see and to let them know you are grateful for them. You can set up reminders in this app as well, making it more useful.

For: iOS Phones
Cost: Free
Website: http://www.begratefulapp.com

Grateful (iOS)

This app reminds you to take time out of each day and note things around you for which you are grateful. Taking some time to reflect on the good in your life will brighten your day a little. With a journal to write in, daily quotes, sharing abilities, and photos, Grateful will make being a thankful person as easy as using an app.

For: iOS Phones
Cost: Free
Website: http://fhands.com/hKe2nrT

Grateful (Windows)

This app is a simple and easy-to-use gratitude journal, right on your phone, a digital journal you can take anywhere and write down the things for which you are grateful. Keeping a gratitude journal is a great way to focus on what makes you happy. Now your journal can go wherever you go. And this digital journal is easy to pull up when you need a little help remembering all the good in your life.

For: Windows Phones
Cost: Free
Website: https://www.microsoft.com/en-us/store/apps/think-grateful/9wzdncrdxs70

Gratitude 365

This app is a great and easy way for you to take some time each day and write down all the things in your life for which you are grateful. Gratitude 365 can become part of your daily routine to focus on all those positive things in your life. You can create a daily list, add pictures, and share your items. You can start or end your day with a note of gratitude, thanks to this app.

For: iOS Phones
Cost: $1.99
Website: http://www.gratitude365app.com

Gratitude Journal

This app has been called life-changing. Not only is it a gratitude journal but it can link to all your devices for easy access and use. It has a traditional feature, if you like the paper-and-pen format, so you feel like you are writing in a book. It also includes different fonts, ratings, a new quote each day, multiple add-ins for each day, and photos you can attach to your list. This app is highly rated, fun, and easy to use as you keep looking for the positive things in life.

For: iOS Phones
Cost: $2.99
Website: https://itunes.apple.com/us/app/gratitude-journal-life-changing/id402667476?mt=8

Gratitude & Happiness

This #1 self-help app is great for keeping track of things that you are grateful for and that make you happy. From a gratitude journal to your degree of happiness to acts of kindness, this app makes being grateful easy. It is simple to share with others as well. You can enter lists, create graphs from past use, and revisit things that have made you happy. Not only does it focus on gratitude but it also focuses on how that affects your happiness. It will help you remember to be grateful and see how much happier you feel when you do.

For: iOS Phones
Cost: $4.99
Website: https://itunes.apple.com/us/app/gratitude-happiness-self-help/id400152780?mt=8

Once you've written down or typed into your app the three things you're thankful for, celebrate! Give yourself a pat on the back for taking one more step toward achieving your goals of inner peace and happiness. I'm proud of you and want you to be proud of you too.

Notes:

_____

_____

_____

_____

_____

_____

_____

Day 9

Dumping Guilt for Good

Recap

We've committed to our happiness goal, are expressing self-love, keeping a gratitude journal, visiting our happiness vision board twice daily, and evaluating our thoughts (without judgment) to replace negative ones with positive ones.

Yesterday we talked about being grateful for all the many blessings we have in our lives. We talked about the importance of finding pleasure in the small things that ultimately bring joy and give life meaning. We practiced being grateful, and hopefully you downloaded an app or two to remind you to be more grateful on a daily basis.

Today we're going focus on eliminating guilt about our illness and understanding how truly special we are. By dumping guilt for good, we'll reduce stress, strain, and ultimately achieve more happiness and fulfillment.

What Is Guilt?

To eliminate this thing called guilt, we first need to understand exactly what guilt is. Check your Merriam-Webster's dictionary for the formal definition, but basically guilt is a feeling of wrongdoing.

By mere definition, **guilt is feeling bad about something we have done to another person.**

However, when you really think about it, your chronic illness **isn't something that you did to someone else. In fact, it's not something that you did to yourself either**. It is merely a part of you and doesn't define you. Say that with me again. "Our chronic illness isn't something we did to ourselves or to someone else."

You can't control it, and you shouldn't allow it to paralyze you with shame. You didn't choose your condition, and you are doing everything you can to feel better, so, why, oh, why should you allow yourself to feel bad about it? Why should you allow your condition to strip you of your dignity or confidence?

Interestingly, most chronic illness warriors understand this on a conscious level, but they have a hard time accepting it on a subconscious level. In our hearts, we know that we shouldn't feel guilty about our illness—after all, we didn't cause it.

Feeling Bad When We Shouldn't

However, our minds tell us that we should feel bad about all the issues our illness causes for others.

For instance, if you're a parent, you might feel guilty because you can't attend school functions, don't have enough energy or stamina to play ping-pong with your kids or to engage in other activities. As a friend, you might feel guilt for canceling plans and not visiting others you care about. As a lover, you might feel guilty about not being able to display romance as frequently as you'd like.

The point is that you must eliminate guilt on a conscious and subconscious level to experience true freedom.

It's OK to feel sad because our lives are different, but it's not OK to dwell on this unhappiness. It's OK to have moments of frustration when we're in a painful flare-up or simply don't feel good; however, it's not OK to stay in this negative frame of mind.

If you don't change your thinking, these negative thoughts can lead to extreme emotional turmoil, and it can be hard (if not impossible) to break this pattern.

When you're chronically ill, you probably experience life's ups and downs. You have some good days, some bad ones, and some average ones. This realization can cause you to feel as if you're on an emotional roller coaster.

To break through this, you must recognize feelings of guilt. For me, I feel it in the pit of my stomach that leads to even more feelings of shame and guilt. If I don't get a handle on it quickly, these emotions can turn into a pity party about how bad life is and how unfair things are. By focusing on all the "*should haves*" and "*could haves*" and "*if onlys*," I feel so dark, desolate, and alone. Not a fun place to be at all.

However, by reminding myself that my illness is not my fault, that I didn't cause it, then it becomes easier to stop these negative feelings once I experience them.

Strategy for Guilt-Free Success

Here are some other tips for dealing with nasty guilt.

Be honest with yourself. Do you have a legitimate reason to feel guilty? Did you genuinely cause yourself or someone else harm? For instance, did you hurt someone's feelings because you were not feeling well and lashed out at them in anger? Did you lie about your illness to get out of an event because you didn't want to see someone you despise?

If you did something wrong, admit it, ask for forgiveness, and move on. On the other hand, if you don't have a reason to feel guilty, then drop those negative feelings now. Remind yourself that these negative feelings have been created by your mind, and the longer you dwell on it, the harder it will be to break free. If you don't, you risk harming your peace of mind and your emotional well-being.

What you need to do next.

Emotional Healing Exercises. These can be helpful when dealing with feelings of guilt. Examples: writing a letter to yourself about your guilty feelings and burning it to let go of those negative emotions. Drawing a picture of what you feel like and then one of how you would like to feel. This can help release your negative emotions of guilt. Even punching a pillow can rid you of negative emotions physically.

Visualization. Visualize yourself in a peaceful, beautiful place in nature. Imagine yourself in the distance and slowly walk toward yourself, until you meet halfway. Now pass yourself a symbol of your forgiveness, maybe a flower or a leaf or anything you like. Realize that your feelings of guilt are just an experience. It could provide you with growth and wisdom.

Once you have handed over your forgiveness symbol, speak to your other self. Don't judge yourself, and speak with love and compassion. Tell yourself that you forgive yourself, and imagine you are now free of your guilt as you hold your symbol in your hands. You can also visualize your guilty feelings as a cloud or a bird. Once you release these feelings and thoughts, you watch them blow away.

Self-Forgiveness. Most people are hard on themselves, and self-forgiveness is not easy to do. First, realize that feeling guilty can keep you stuck in the negativity of the past. Accepting the past, while knowing you cannot change it, is the first step. Next remind yourself that negative emotions will drain your physical energy and affect your overall health and well-being.

You must let go of those negative emotions to be healthier. Understand that forgiving yourself doesn't mean you need to always fix things; sometimes you can't or don't need to. And you can forgive yourself without involving anyone else. Lastly, once you learn to forgive yourself, you are energetically releasing yourself from the guilty feelings that have been pulling you down.

Daily Exercise

Repeat after me: "I didn't cause my illness, and I shouldn't feel guilty about it. Guilt and shame will only win if I allow them to. I choose to be in control of any guilty feelings and to see the best in my life and my situation. I chose happiness now."

Today's Activity:

Take a few minutes and answer the following three questions.

What are five things I feel guilty about?

_____

_____

_____

_____

_____

Why do I feel so guilty?

_____

_____

_____

_____

_____

_____

What are some things I can do now about these guilty feelings and when they pop up in the future?

_____

_____

_____

_____

_____

_____

Don't let guilt of any kind eat away at you and cause you more pain and stress when you don't need it. If you are creating the reasons behind your guilt, you need to recognize these negative thoughts and stop them before they become a bigger burden.

Guilt can impact your physical health and mental well-being, so learning and practicing how to relieve yourself of these feelings will only improve your life. **Remember you are worthy of your own forgiveness and love.**

Day 10

Take Control of Negative Emotions and Prepare for Better Days Ahead

Recap

With your commitment to happiness, self-love, gratitude, squashing negative thoughts and encouraging positive ones, eliminating guilt from your mind, you must continue to resist the urge to feel guilty—even a little bit. Otherwise you're back to square one before you even made progress!

Every time those guilty feelings creep in, try some of the methods we mentioned previously: visualization; self-forgiveness; natural remedies, like Bach Flower essences; etc. You must do what you need to do to push those negative thoughts from your mind. Learn how to focus on feeling at peace and being happy moment by moment.

Why Is This Important?

The moment that you learn to take control of your emotions, you can change your inner world. The moment you feel as if you can turn off guilt, negativity, condemnation, and fear **is the moment when you ultimately take back your power.**

Consider two warriors, Betty and Bonnie. Which of the stories below sounds familiar? Who would you want to be known as?

Betty was diagnosed with depression and lupus over ten years ago. Although she experiences frequent pain flare-ups and bouts of depression, and spends most of her days in bed**, she has not given up hope** and is committed to getting better and living a happier life. Before Betty learned to control guilt and to focus on the positive aspects of her life, she felt worse. She felt disconnected from the world around her and also felt as if she had no life.

Then **she had a mind shift.** She realized that the only person she was hurting with this defeatist attitude was herself. Nothing much has changed regarding her physical condition, yet she feels better and stronger emotionally. She feels as if her life has improved tremendously. Although she still spends a lot of time in bed, she has learned to appreciate a good book. She has also learned to stay connected to family and friends via social media and personalized letters and emails. She has learned to do what she can with the life she has been given. She has learned to live life to the fullest right from her bedside.

Bonnie, on the other hand, was also diagnosed with lupus and depression over five years ago. Although she takes medication to prevent pain flare-ups and works hard to control her depression, **she often delves into weeklong pity parties about how awful her life is**. This tends to alienate those close to her. Like Betty, Bonnie spends a lot of time in bed and doesn't feel very well. In fact, she typically has more bad days than good ones. She isn't able to visit friends or go out much. However, she has decided that she would rather just not put forth the effort and take her life for what it is.

When people try to connect with her, Bonnie ignores them and falls deeper into a sense of depression from her lack of meaningful relationships. She spends her life with the covers pulled over her head because she simply just wants life to end. In reality, Bonnie's illnesses have taken over her life. She is allowing them to define her. She is enabling guilt, frustration, and anger to get in the way of her true happiness.

It's clear which one is leading the optimal life. You probably already know that. So what's holding you back? *You.* That's why your mission today is to gain a sense of control over your emotions and to make positive changes in your life so that you can feel better about the life you have been given. Although you can't control all the aspects of your illness, **you can make good of the life that you have now and make it happier.**

You may not be able to do the things you once did, but you can do some cool things.

Write down five things you can no longer do anymore due to your medical challenge.

_____
_____
_____
_____
_____

Write down how you feel about not being able to do those things.

_____
_____
_____
_____

Write down five things that you can do right now to bring happiness and fulfillment to your life.

_____
_____
_____
_____
_____

What you need to do to change your future is in the following paragraphs.

You'll be more successful at stemming those pangs of guilt and woe-is-me feelings if you get a better sense of when (and why) those feelings start.

Today's Activity:

Do feel guilt and/or pity yourself after seeing photos of other people having fun outside? Is it after watching a movie with happy people in it? Is it something to do with your family?

Make a point to write down a quick note when you feel that old familiar feeling creeping in. Do this a few times and see what pattern emerges, then choose a strategy to help avoid those situations. Knowledge offers control. You can't curb a bad habit if you don't understand how it starts!

Day 11

Committing to Put Yourself First

Recap

We are at the halfway mark, having set up a good foundation. Yesterday we learned how to better control negative emotions. We learned how to listen to our thoughts and to change our world. Today we're focusing on the importance of giving ourselves the love and support we need to grow and flourish!

Self-preservation is so important. Think about it—even airplane companies understand this phenomenon. Just remember the last time you flew on a plane. Do you remember the advice given by the flight attendants? They likely said, "Put your oxygen mask on first so that you can help others. If you run out of oxygen, you can't help anyone."

Well, that same advice applies to our daily life. You cannot pour from an empty cup. Believe me. I've tried.

As chronic illness warriors, we're all predisposed to put others' needs before our own. Our kids, our spouse, our aging parents—they all come first. It's just what we do. We nurture; we nurture, and we nurture until we're empty physically and mentally.

At some point though we must take care of our own needs and our own happiness. We must put our needs first. We must demonstrate with our actions that we love ourselves as much as—if not more than—we love others. **We can't simply say yes every time someone asks us to do something**, especially if we're not up to doing whatever they're requesting. We have to put our well-being and happiness first, and shouldn't worry what other people think. We should care more about what we think.

Spending all our available time and resources on everyone else's needs means neglecting our own. When you consistently put others' needs before your own, you ignore the little nagging signs that tell you to stop and breathe. You know the signs. They show up in the form of having more aggravating symptoms; being more tired and irritable; getting more emotional, more easily frustrated.

All this giving eventually leads to you giving out. This is a sure sign that you need to stop and pay attention to you.

These physical and emotional symptoms are your body's way of getting your attention. It may start slowly, but, if you don't pay attention to it, you could find yourself emotionally and physically drained, and then you won't be able to care for yourself or anyone else for that matter.

So, if this describes you, where exactly do you begin? How do you turn it around and fit your self-care into your already busy day? You do it slowly, one step at a time.

Here are a few things you can do each day to start putting your happiness first:

- **Carve out thirty minutes each day to do something that makes you happy.** It could be painting, cooking, sewing, gardening, or even just taking a long hot bath. The point is to dedicate thirty minutes of your day to you.

- **Journal**. Sometimes writing down all that's going on in your life can help you get to the root of what you truly want to do in your life. It's very meditative and therapeutic.
- **Avoid junk food.** Food is fuel for the body. If you're taking care of others all day, you're already burning the candle at both ends. It's important that you at least nourish your body with healthy and healing food. Foods like turkey, pineapples, tofu, nuts, and seeds naturally raise serotonin (a neurotransmitter involved in the control of the sleep-wake cycle, mood levels, and pain management).

Today's Activities:

Commit to putting yourself first.

Say out loud: "Today, and everyday hereafter, I will take time for myself. I will put my needs first. I will do those things that make me happy. I will ensure that I am better equipped to do all I want to do, including taking care of those I love."

Write down five things you've been putting off that you really want to do for yourself:

1. _____
2. _____
3. _____
4. _____
5. _____

Get out your calendar, planner, or both, and mark off five days this month when you will complete the above activities, no matter what! Then ensure you do them.

Say No to Guilt!

Day 12

Following Through on Your Commitment to Self

Recap

Having established a good foundation in the first ten days, yesterday we talked about the importance of putting your needs first. We talked about how you should love yourself unconditionally and not be afraid to say no to others. We also talked about how hard it is to stay committed to ourselves.

Today I'd like to provide you with a battle plan for when you're tempted to ignore the advice from the previous chapter.

In your heart, you now know making a real binding commitment to put ourselves first and to prioritize our dreams of health, happiness, and inner peace is important. You know taking tiny actions every single day to make your dreams a reality is also necessary and important. But somehow it doesn't happen.

You Need to Follow-Through

Just like you set goals and work toward accomplishing them, you also need to work on following through with your own commitments to you. Life will inevitably throw you some curves. Live long enough and it will happen. But what will you do about it?

Hopefully you'll remember that you matter very much. Hopefully you'll relinquish thoughts that you should sacrifice your happiness for the greater good of mankind. Although this sounds nice and dandy and is somewhat ingrained in your brain, this type of thinking often leads to unhappiness and frustration.

On one hand, we know putting others' happiness before our own is senseless, but we feel guilty when we don't. Therefore, you must stay committed to making yourself happy even when you feel guilty about doing so. You must consistently remind yourself that you are the most important person and that taking care of yourself is neither selfish nor makes you a bad person.

Instead you must feel it in your core that you are doing the right thing.

Here are five ideas to help you stay committed to meeting your own needs before you meet other people's needs:

1. **Understand that putting your needs first is not selfish.** You are the most important person in your life. You know your likes and dislikes better than anyone else, and you also know how to make yourself happy. By purposely putting other people's needs first, you set the stage for negative emotions to flow out of you, which is not good for you or anyone else.

2. *No* **is a powerful word. Use it.** Knowing your mental and physical limitations and not going beyond them will go a long way to securing your happiness. When family members, friends, or colleagues put unrealistic expectations on you, tell them no. If you don't, you won't have the time or energy to get the things done that you need to do. You especially must say no when other people's needs contradict yours.

3. **Be mindful of how you treat yourself.** Your happiness is just as important as anyone else's happiness. In fact, if truth be told, your happiness should be the most important thing for you. If you don't feel happy and content, then you certainly can't be happy and content, and you can't share these positive feelings with others. You can't give what you haven't got.

4. **Drop guilt.** As we discussed previously, guilt has no place in your life. When others try to guilt you into doing something you don't want to do, realize what they're doing and refuse to acknowledge their manipulations.

5. **Take small steps every day.** You don't have to change all at once. Make small commitments to putting yourself first every day and soon it will become a habit.

Today's Activities:

Think of any other ideas to keep you focused on your commitment to yourself and write them down.

_____

_____

_____

_____

_____

Next take this pledge: "I am committed to myself. I will not let others deter me from my goals of making myself happy. I am important. I love, admire, and respect myself. I matter, and I must put my needs first. I must take care of me before I can even think about taking care of anyone else."

Do something special for yourself that you've wanted to do for a while now. Maybe something that you planned to do another day this month. Well, do it today instead.

Notes:

_____

_____

_____

_____

_____

_____

_____

_____

_____

_____

_____

Day 13

Recognizing Happiness-Stealers

Recap

Yesterday we talked about happiness and the importance of reprioritizing your actions so that your needs are met. Although you can control your actions and can put an end to how you perceive your condition, you may find other people are your happiness-drainers, making you worry, comparing yourself to others, and more. Today we'll provide you with tools to recognize and to get rid of people like that in your life.

What most people discover is that they aren't nearly as much of the problem as others around them. Some people will wear you down, if you allow them to. If you have these types of people in your life, time to let go of these extraneous happiness-and peace-drainers now. Once and for all.

So being happy means you must recognize happiness-stealers around you. This is especially true because living with chronic illness can make it difficult to maintain a happy-go-lucky disposition or even a pleasant one! But you have the power to change your life. You have the power to stop happiness-stealers in their tracks. You have the power to achieve more happiness than you've ever dreamed of, and you can do it now.

First, you have to steer clear of your own happiness-stealers before they diminish your overall sense of contentment over time. Here are some of the most common happiness-stealers:

1. Focusing on everyone else's story. Although it is good to be motivated by the success of other chronic illness warriors, don't be so satisfied with the success stories of others and how things have gone for them that you forget to write your own. Just like others, you too have everything you need to become what you are capable of. You are special, unique. Your life has purpose. You will experience incredible and positive changes in your life when you take control of your life. By dreaming big and being willing to put forth a bit of effort into making those dreams a reality, you can achieve everything you want to achieve.

If you want your life story to soar to new heights, you've got to clear a path, reduce the time-sinks and burdens weighing you down, and pick up the things that give you wings. Keep your best wishes and your biggest goals close to your heart, and dedicate time to them every single day. Even if you have to force yourself to get it done, do it because making a commitment to yourself and keeping it with those small mundane activities is what changes thoughts into action. If you truly care about your goals, and you work diligently at achieving them every day, there's almost nothing you can't accomplish.

2. Waiting for the perfect moment. So many people wait around for the stars to align to do what they're here to do. However, they sadly realize that this may never happen, and their dreams fall by the wayside. **Don't buy into the myth of the perfect moment.** Moments aren't perfect; they're what you make them.

Your ability to grow to your highest potential is directly related to your willingness to act in the face of imperfection. You will succeed not by finding a perfect moment but by learning to see and to use life's imperfections perfectly. Act; don't wait. Waiting is stalling, and you know it.

3. Holding tight to worries and fears. Someday, when you look back over your life, you'll realize that nearly all your worries and anxious fears never came to fruition. They were completely unfounded. When you look at the last few years, how many opportunities for joy were destroyed by needless worry and negativity? How many times have you talked yourself out of doing something because it was too much work? If so, stop right now.

Although there's nothing you can do about these lost joys, there's plenty you can do about the ones still to come. You can take control of your life, but first you must let go of fear and worry.

4. Dwelling on difficulties. A bad day is just a bad day. Choose not to make it anything more. Times of adversity will inevitably affect the conditions in which you live and work; yet you don't have to let it affect who you are and where you're headed. Take note of the setbacks and adjust to them but don't expand them by making them a bigger part of your life.

Every day brings new lessons and new possibilities. There is always a way to take the next step forward on the path you've chosen. Events may be terrible and inescapable at times, but you always have a choice—if not *when*, then *how* you may endure and proceed onward.

5. Holding on to someone who hurts you. Sometimes you have to walk away from people (even family members), not because you don't care about them, but because you care more about yourself and your feelings, and are tired of being hurt. As chronic illness warriors, it's hard because you are often dealing with an invisible illness that others can't see or feel. And oftentimes they simply can't give you the compassion or support you need. Instead of internalizing this, love them and let them go. Realize that they aren't able to give you the level of respect and love you deserve, and it's OK. By letting them go, you release them to their highest good, and you protect yourself. It's a tough pill to swallow, but it's necessary medicine.

Today's Activities:

Here are some activities to help you recognize the happiness stealers in your life:

1. For one week, keep a detailed log of how you spend your time. Write down details about your mood and what caused you to feel the way you do. If something brings you down, note it and how you can handle similar situations in the future. At the end you might be surprised by how much time you spent *consuming* that you could've spent *creating*.

2. Think of something you've wanted to do for a while that relates to your passion that you've been putting off. Write down five reasons why you should do the one thing that you've been putting off and how you can overcome this procrastination for good. Commit to doing one manageable thing this week that will bring you closer to achieving that goal.

Here's an affirmation you should say five times into the mirror each morning:

"I will not dwell on the bad in life. Instead I will focus my energy on the good."

Day 14

Letting Go of Happiness-and Peace-Drainers

Recap

Now that we've mastered how to put your needs first, and you can recognize happiness stealers (whether your own procrastination or added stress from someone else), today you need an action plan on how to handle negative people and situations.

After all, it is great to put yourself first, but you don't live in a bubble, and people will either build you up or tear you down. The key is to surround yourself with people who will help and to steer clear of those who won't.

Today's Lesson: Don't Make Life Tougher Than It Already Is

Dealing with a chronic illness is hard enough, and, when you have unsupportive happiness-and peace-drainers unloading their crap onto you, it can be even harder to cope. This isn't to say that you should X out everyone in your life. No one is perfect, and we all have issues. However, if you're constantly around people draining what little energy and happiness you have left, it is time to let them go.

I admit that this isn't easy to do, especially if these happiness-and peace-drainers are family and close friends, but it is absolutely crucial for you to limit time with them or to make a conscious effort to not engage with them at all.

But how can you figure out who needs the ax? It's really not as hard as it seems. If you feel anxious or depressed when you're around them, if their presence maxes out the last bit of energy you have, if their unnecessary demands and wants cause you added stress, they should definitely be put on the list.

Here are some other ways to recognize a happiness- and/or peace-drainer:

1. They don't tend to take a real interest in you. Everything is a prelude to talking about themselves. If you tell them that you have chronic migraines and ultimately don't feel well, they tell you that they had a terrible headache once but took some Tylenol and now feel better. Another example: they ask how you're doing in the first thirty seconds to a minute of their call, and, before you've really had a chance to say anything at all, they've swung back to what they really want to talk about—themselves.

2. They don't have levels, only extremes. If you imagine drama and how you respond to it on a scale of one to five, with three being middle of the road and four to five being serious cause for concern, everything to these people is a five or a twenty. This makes it difficult to know what to take seriously. For instance, everything from a stubbed toe to a flat tire is a major catastrophe that demands that you stop everything to help.

3. They don't take responsibility. Even if they keep telling variations of the same story, just with different people, it's everyone else who's the problem. These people also see it as your responsibility to make them feel better, which is why they feel indignant if you won't drop everything to do so. For instance, let's say that you don't feel well, and your happiness-drainer demands that you see them right away because they're sad about a recent breakup. You tell them that you love and support them, and will administer phone support, but you can't get out right now. They then proceed to tell you that you're a terrible friend because you won't drop everything right now to help them.

4. The road does not go both ways. When you have your own stuff going on, you're met with tumbleweeds or dismissed with what can be a scary lack of empathy. It's also possible that, when you have an issue, they're nowhere to be seen. For instance, you receive a diagnosis that you have a chronic illness, like fibromyalgia. Your peace-drainer tells you that they heard that aloe vera juice will cure your ailment and that you should just stop complaining so much because everyone hurts. Argh!

What to Do?

If any of these sound like someone in your life, what can you do to let go of these happiness-and peace-drainers?

1. Be honest about who the drainers are in your life. Protect your own well-being. Note how your body feels, your thoughts, your emotions, the typical situations involved, and let these be your warning signals so that you can take care of yourself.

2. Set a time limit for engagement. Don't hold yourself hostage on calls or in situations. Say how long you've got when they get on the phone and stick to it. No more than ten to fifteen minutes. Then give them a couple minutes' warning before you're due to go and, no matter how much they try to plow on, be firm and tell them you have to go and say bye. It's a healthy way of setting boundaries without getting into a big discussion.

3. Let them get on with their own lives. Conversations with drainers are not about you providing a solution; it's about telling them what they want to hear and/or letting them listen to their own voice. Listen with boundaries—don't stress yourself out trying to find the solution or to be the solution. "I'm sorry to hear that" or "I really hope you get it sorted out soon" are easy replacements for trying to rack your brain.

Today's Activities:

Remember that you can be empathetic and supportive—honor your boundaries with compassion. These people are obviously going through their own stuff but don't project or cross your own or their boundaries by making you responsible for changing their feelings and behavior.

Here's an **affirmation** you can say in front of the mirror each morning as you try to get rid of the happiness-and peace-drainers in your life:

"It is not my responsibility to shoulder the burdens of others. It is my responsibility to take care of myself. I will continue to put my needs and happiness first."

Day 15

Getting the Support You Need from Loved Ones

Yesterday we talked about the importance of getting rid of peace-and happiness-drainers. We discussed how to spot these people and what to do about them. By now you have probably short-listed a few candidates and created an action plan to deal with them. Good for you. I know it wasn't easy, but it is definitely worth the effort.

Having a chronic illness can feel extremely lonely at times. You may even feel as if no one gets you or the struggles you experience on a daily basis. In all honesty, it can be hard for people who don't have a chronic illness to truly understand what you're going through.

Yes, they may be empathetic, and they may see you suffering, but they may not get how much you struggle day in and day out for better health. They may not see that you need support and understanding as much as you need water, food, and air. So, time to get the support you need from loved ones.

How to Get the Support You Need

So today we will focus on reconnecting with family and friends whose friendships you've taken for granted or dropped because they simply weren't able to understand you and your illness.

By reaching out to them with an open heart and understanding, and doing so without expectations, **you are offering acceptance**.

By reconciling with those whom you've had problems with in the past, forgiving them and showing that you will not carry resentment, guilt, or shame in you, **you will feel free**.

By replacing anger and frustration with unconditional love, **you set the stage for real support to begin**.

The key, however, is to go about it without expectations. You can't demand that they comprehend or understand you. But you can request that they be more understanding. You can reach out and extend the olive branch without expecting anything in return. You can reach out with hope because, simply put, it feels good to have actual human beings who can talk with you and hug you and spend time with you, without the Web between you.

Yes, we'll discuss virtual friendships too, but today we will focus on real human connections. Online forums and social media conversations can't replace having someone who can offer a hug, who can look into your eyes and see you are hurting, or who can sit and listen as you mentally process what you're going through.

Make sure you spend time alone with all the important people in your life, particularly your partner and your children. Develop a closer relationship with each member of your immediate family, and you will all have an easier time coping with the disease.

Tips for Support System Success

- Write a letter telling your loved ones how you feel and what you expect from them in terms of support.

- Ask your doctor to explain your condition to those who you love and care about in a way that they'll truly understand.

- Purchase a few books about your specific illness and ask your family and friends to read through them.

- Watch movies with loved ones about people with similar conditions so that your family and friends will be more empathetic.

- Accept them for what they can give, hold your head up, and know that you can and will get the support you deserve.

Whatever you do, don't expect too much. It's true that your family and friends love and care about you but are not able to comprehend exactly what you're going through. That is, they can only give you a certain amount of support. If you need more, then don't be afraid to ask for it.

Today's Activities:

Please write down a list of five people who are important to you and the reason you're not as connected as you used to be.

1. _____
2. _____
3. _____
4. _____
5. _____

Name five ways you can connect with each person today.

1. _____
2. _____
3. _____
4. _____
5. _____

Say No to Guilt!

Day 16

Discover an Online Support Network

Recap

Yesterday we talked about asking your friends and family members for support. How did it go? Did you take the first step toward building a support system? I know it may have been daunting and maybe a little scary to put yourself out there, but, then again, it's even scarier to do this all alone. It's worth the effort. I promise you.

Perhaps you had some frank talks with your friends and family about your needs or shared a movie with them. Either way, now put together another group of like-minded warriors to help you on your quest for better health, happiness, and peace. Connect with those who are exactly where you are.

Finding an Online Community That Gets You

Today we will focus on evaluating the many options that chronic illness warriors have access to for seeking support from other warriors like you. For instance, social media networks are a great way for you to connect with others with similar issues and for you to share your feelings in an open and supportive environment. I've made some really great friends on Twitter (@successthang), Instagram, Pinterest, Facebook Groups, and more. The really amazing thing is that you don't have to explain your condition because these people totally get what you're going through.

They won't recommend that you get more rest, try a concoction of apple cider vinegar or "special juice" to cure you or anything like that. If we all had a nickel for every time some distant relative heard about some "magical cure" on some talk show, we would be rich!

Instead these online people will understand and relate to your daily struggles as a chronic illness warrior, offer advice and support when needed, and soft gentle hugs when needed too. Speaking of which, here's a hug from me to you. I'm so very glad you're doing something to improve your life, and—trust me—I *get you.*

To help you with your efforts, here are a few sites that you may want to check out. To make it easier, I've broken these support networks down into types of chronic illnesses. However, this is certainly not an exhaustive list, and, if you don't find a group you relate to, don't give up. You can certainly find another and another and another.

The important thing is that you don't give up and that you keep searching for a group that gels well with you, your personality, and your desires. More important, avoid groups who don't seem like they support their members and/or who are more focused on complaining than truly helping and listening. You don't need negativity like that! We already spent a few chapters getting rid of those notions. Find a community of members who helps you feel like you have a team.

Chronic Illness Sites

Arthritis

Inspire Arthritis Support Group

https://www.inspire.com/groups/arthritis-foundation/

Arthritis support group and discussion community.

SupportGroups.com

http://arthritis.supportgroups.com/

The Arthritis Support Group is here for anyone looking for support in dealing with arthritis. You can join the Arthritis Support Groups here for free.

Spine Health Arthritis Forum

http://www.spine-health.com/forum/categories/arthritis-osteoarthritis

For discussions focused on arthritis.

Diabetes

DiabetesForum.com

http://www.diabetesforum.com/forum.php

The diabetes support forum has the latest news and discussions on symptoms, treatments, monitoring, diets, and research.

Diabetic Community

http://diabeticnetwork.com/community/

Huge site dedicated to discussing diabetes. Manage diabetes by discussing it with others. Perfect for newly diagnosed diabetics.

Cancer

Cancer Survivors Network

http://csn.cancer.org/?_ga=1.228479581.1372231027.1458998757

Network of survivors. Membership is free, but, in order to access all areas of CSN, registration with a valid email address is required.

ACOR.ORG

http://www.acor.org/#browse

Features information, treatments, links, and provides online community support for a wide range of different types of cancer.

Lupus

Daily Strength

http://www.dailystrength.org/c/Lupus/support-group

Dedicated Lupus Support Group with health information to help educate and empower those who suffer with lupus.

MD Junction

http://www.mdjunction.com/lupus

The MD Junction Lupus Support Group is a community of patients, family members, and friends dedicated to dealing with lupus, together.

WebMD

http://exchanges.webmd.com/lupus-exchange

If you or a loved one are living with lupus, then get support, information, and treatment options from experts and other members here.

Fibromyalgia

My Fibro Team

https://www.myfibroteam.com/

The social network and support group for those living with fibromyalgia.

Daily Strength

http://www.dailystrength.org/c/Fibromyalgia/support-group

Daily strength for fibromyalgia with community advisors.

Chronic Migraines

Migraine Support Group - Facebook

https://www.facebook.com/MigraineSupport/ - "Like" the Page

The Migraine Support Group page exists to provide an informational and cohesive community for people suffering from chronic migraine attacks.

WebMD

http://exchanges.webmd.com/migraines-and-headaches-exchange

WebMD migraines and headaches community.

Heart Disease

Support Network

http://supportnetwork.heart.org/home

Designed for stroke and heart patients and caregivers. Improve your life and the lives of others when you join the American Heart Association/American Stroke Association Support Network. Share your experiences; give and get emotional support. If you are the caregiver, there are others just like you who can help.

SupportGroups.com

http://www.supportgroups.com/support-groups/all-support-group-posts

The Heart Attack Support Group is here for anyone looking for support in dealing with a heart attack. You can join the Heart Attack Support Group here for free.

Chronic Respiratory Diseases

Daily Strength

http://www.dailystrength.org/support-groups/Lungs-Respiration

Meet others online who are facing challenges related to lungs and respiration. Get support by sharing advice, trading tips, and telling your story.

Inspire

https://www.inspire.com/groups/american-lung-association-lung-disease/

Lung infections and diseases support group and discussion community.

By connecting with like-minded people, you will be able to not only read their personal stories of challenges and triumphs but you'll see that you are NOT alone. Others have experienced similar situations like you and are living a victorious life.

Today's Activity:

Find five online support groups specifically for your chronic illness and visit them today. Pick two of those groups and make an introductory post about yourself with a brief background. You'll be surprised how many people will understand your experience!

Say No to Guilt!

Day 17

Setting SMART Goals for Chronic Illness Warriors

Recap

Now that you have put your needs first and have a support group in place, you should be more committed, focused, and happier.

Today we will discuss motivation and goal achievement.

I've said it once already. I'll say it one thousand times more. Life with chronic pain is a life of constant struggles. A struggle to avoid pain. A struggle to remain positive. A struggle to have a peaceful and meaningful life right now. A struggle to make every day count. I get it! I truly do! And I also get that those struggles mustn't define you because then they will define your goals.

If you're like most high achievers, you have plenty of short-and long-term goals. Some you've been able to complete, and some you've put on the back burner simply because you don't have the energy to get it done. These goals may involve managing pain, maximizing sleep, exercising, eating healthy meals, or simply being happy. However, resolving to exercise more, eat better, get more sleep, etc., does not turn into efforts with lasting results. Why? Because a goal that is not SMART doesn't get accomplished. If it were as easy as saying, "Get more sleep," then wouldn't we all be well-rested?

When you set SMART goals for yourself, you set yourself up for success not failure. A SMART goal is one that is:

- Specific

- Measurable

- Attainable

- Relevant

- Timely

Specific versus General

The problem with warriors who set nonspecific goals—like, I need to exercise more or eat better—is that those goals are too general. When they're undefined, you just don't push yourself to get them done. Instead you put them off and put them off until days, months, and years have passed, and then you wonder, where did the time go?

The best way to think about setting goals is to think like an award-winning journalist would attack an article.

Ask yourself:

- Who is involved?

- What do I want to accomplish?

- Where will it take place?

- When will it take place?

- Why am I doing this?

- How to best do this to get the results I desire?

Make your goals as specific as possible. Instead of saying you'll exercise more, resolve to walk one thousand steps a day, two days a week. Instead of vowing to eat better, resolve to limit sugary snacks to one per day. Instead of promising to sleep more, resolve to go to bed a 9:30 p.m. every night (including weekends). And write it down in a visible spot!

Measure Your Goals

Once you've set up this goal, your work is not done. You now need to measure what you're trying to achieve, or you'll never know when you're done. Ask yourself:

- How much?

- How many?

- How will I know when my goal is accomplished?

Set Attainable Goals

Make sure that your goal is something you can realistically achieve in the amount of time you've given yourself. Like the saying goes, "Rome wasn't built in a day." Setting unrealistic goals is simply setting yourself up for failure and disappointment. And, if you want to achieve inner peace and happiness, you must set yourself up for success. A popular business saying used by companies like Zappos is "undersell, overdeliver." Set a realistic goal and then zoom past it.

Make Sure Your Goals Are Relevant

Next you'll need to stay laser-focused on the "why" of your goal that we talked about above. If you can't pinpoint exactly why you want to accomplish the goal in the first place, you likely won't do so. It has to be compelling so you want to do it!

Set Deadlines for Yourself and Stick to Them

You can set all the most beautifully well-thought-out goals you want, and they won't mean anything if you don't have a deadline. It's easy to resolve to lose ten pounds if you don't have any end date in sight. Resolving to lose ten pounds by August 31, conversely, will give you focus and a finish line to race toward.

Today's Activities:

Here are a few activities for you to practice today and every day hereafter:

- Each morning when you wake up, make a list of three to five goals to accomplish. Then pick the one you absolutely need to do and tackle that first. Vow to get that one thing done and do it first, before you move on to any other goals on the list.

- Keep a written log of your progress. It will help to motivate you!

- Meditate for ten to twenty minutes before you start your task. This will increase your self-awareness, which will in turn help you to notice when negative thoughts threaten to get in the way of you achieving your goals.

Remember that, even if you've failed to achieve your goals in the past, the problem was never you. The problem was your approach. With SMART goals you can learn, grow, and create lasting change.

Today's Affirmation:

"Today I will set SMART goals for myself. They will be Specific, Measureable, Attainable, Relevant, and Timely. I will achieve every goal I set out to accomplish in due time. I will feel proud of my accomplishments today and every day."

Notes:

_____

_____

_____

_____

Day 18

Develop a Contingency Plan to Handle Setbacks

Recap

Yesterday we learned about setting SMART goals. We wrote down some goals that we wanted to accomplish. Today we'll develop a contingency plan to handle setbacks.

Let's be very honest with each other. You and I both know this won't always be smooth sailing. That's why, as you go on your journey, you must remember that every day will be different. Some days you'll feel as if you are on top of the world, and other days you'll feel as if the world has stepped on you.

The key is to realize that, although these setbacks will undoubtedly occur, you must simply see them as temporary setbacks and not as permanent obstacles. You must be prepared with an action plan for when things don't go the way you want. That's the difference between thriving and wallowing. We've already done way too much wallowing. Make today different.

For instance, when I was working on this book, I experienced many painful flare-ups, and ended up with a weeklong migraine and the flu. I had a ton of good excuses as to why I couldn't achieve the goal of writing this book, and, on the surface, they all seemed like excellent reasons. But, when I delved deeper, I realized that they were cop-outs. Yes, I didn't feel well. There are weeks when I don't feel well. However, I push on because I know that even pain flare-ups, headaches, and the flu will eventually pass.

My potential disappointment in myself for not following through and keeping my word to myself, on the other hand, will certainly live on. Whenever I don't keep my word to myself, I suffer negative feelings, stress, and turmoil. So I made it a point to write five hundred words every single day, even when I felt like crap. Yes, I probably will go back and rewrite those sections so they are coherent, but that's all part of being an author.

Therefore, today we will focus on creating a contingency action plan when things just don't go as planned. We will discuss what to do when you experience setbacks and will write down your plan for dealing with them—not if, but when, they come up.

If you don't, you will inevitably give into everyday dramas and traumas, and will never experience true happiness and pride from setting a goal and then achieving it head-on. You will never feel the beauty of being proud of yourself when you kept your word and did something you didn't feel like doing.

In fact, most success gurus state that the big actions don't cause the greatest success. Instead those mundane consistent actions you do day in and day out allow you to not only experience peace but achieve true success as well.

Here are some tips for setting up contingency plans.

1. **Do a little bit.** Let's say that you set a goal to walk three thousand steps a day but can't accomplish your daily walk

goal. Instead of verbally beating up yourself and viewing yourself as a loser who can't accomplish her goals, just do as much as you can and drop the guilt. Set a new goal to walk five hundred steps and then ramp it up until you've finally reached your original goal. In a few days, you will feel better, and you'll be able to reach that goal of three thousand steps. The point isn't some arbitrary number or milestone. The point is, you are putting forth all the effort and energy you can muster to accomplish something. There's no shame in that. The shame is in saying, "It's too hard."

2. **Don't beat yourself up about it.** As much as you try, some days you simply can't get done what you planned to do, and that's OK. Perhaps you can still do something that takes a bit less effort but still leads you to your goals. For instance, if I set a goal to get up and wash my hair, and I honestly just don't feel like it, I still comb it and put on clean clothes. I do small things that will make me feel better, even though I can't do the one thing that I want to do.

3. **Plan around those bad days.** When you set up your goals, factor in that you will likely have bad days. Give yourself more time than you need to get things done and vow to eventually get it done, even if you have to put it off for a bit. Assuming every day will go as planned is setting yourself up for failure. It's better to predict a small setback, because then it's not really a setback at all!

4. **Outsource it.** If you just can't complete a task, and you need it done, consider outsourcing it. Sites like Upwork, Fiverr, or TaskRabbit allow you to hire contractors to assist with administrative, website design, social media, personal tasks (like standing in line to get concert tickets, grocery shopping, etc.). In fact, many experts say getting these types of trivial tasks off your plate so you can focus on big picture tasks is the best path for success.

Today's Affirmation: "I am amazing, and I must always put myself first. By planning for situations that I can't control, I stay committed to my goals and happiness."

Today's Activities:

Write down five things you will do if you aren't able to do something you really need to get done.

_____

_____

_____

_____

_____

Day 19

Overcoming Jealousy

Recap

Yesterday we talked about developing contingency plans and how to propel ourselves forward when we experience setbacks. One setback that can put you in a negative place is jealousy. Time to get rid of the green-eyed monster.

Ever seen someone driving down the street in some slick new luxury automobile and thought, "Wow, I'd love to drive that!" Or watched a happy couple walk hand-in-hand, completely in love, when maybe your own love life is lackluster, and pined for what they had?

We've all been there. It's hard not to turn on the TV without being hit over the head with jealousy-driving images.

When suffering from a chronic illness, it's difficult not to feel envious of the people in your life who are in good health. And, unlike the material-driven jealousy we sometimes feel but know doesn't really matter, this kind of envy seems all too real and consequential. You see how they lack your limitations, and their lives seem so easy and unencumbered compared with yours. Perhaps they can eat food you can't or drink alcohol or stay out late into the night. You may wish you could trade places with them so you could lead a free and simple life too.

I'm here to say, stop it.

Stop comparing. Stop playing "What if?" Stop looking at someone else's life as some utopia. It's important not to compare your situation with anyone else's. It won't improve anything about your own situation and will clog your brain with negative thoughts and feelings. You're not thinking of all the positives going on with your life, including some, I bet, those other people wish they had (like your courage and perseverance!)

You can do a few things to avoid these flare-ups of jealousy.

Address Your Jealousy

The first step in dealing with your problem is admitting you have one. Admit to yourself that you are jealous of your friend. Once you give voice to your feelings, those feelings will have less power to control you. Now that you're more aware of your jealousy toward your friend, you'll be more likely to notice any negative thoughts you might be directing toward him or her. You might also realize how much those feelings are overtaking your life.

Practice Self-Care

Jealousy is a stress response, and, if you are already feeling stress in other aspects of your life, you'll more likely experience negative thoughts and feelings. Make sure you eat a healthy diet, exercise to the best of your ability, and get enough sleep. These self-care basics are so important, not only when it comes to keeping a healthy body but a healthy mind. As a bonus, if you do those things, guess what? You'll realize *you* are the one of whom people should be jealous.

Find Joy in the Joy of Others

It can be tempting to focus on what someone else has and you don't in a negative way, wishing to possess what that other person has. However, you can also choose to look at things more positively. Feel glad about your friends' good health. It's OK if you have to fake it at first—eventually the goodwill feelings will become genuine, and your friends will still appreciate the genuine gesture.

Reality Check

You may be convinced that the lives of your healthy friends are so much better than yours, but there's always so much you don't know. Your friends surely have myriad issues of their own that you wouldn't want. As the saying goes, you should never judge a book by its cover. Everyone has something they are dealing with—a family member who passed away, the loss of a job or an unending job search, taking care of kids, and the list goes on.

Today's Affirmations:

Here are a few affirmations you can repeat to yourself each day to help overcome your jealousy:

"I am on my own unique journey, and I will not compare myself to others."

"I am not defined by my illness, and I won't let it hold me back from achieving my dreams."

"I am happy for my friends' good health and do not envy them."

Today's Activities:

One exercise to try is writing each day in a gratitude journal. Recount everything in your life for which you are grateful. This regular practice of thinking positively and writing down those thoughts will help you realize how great your life really is.

Another exercise that could help with jealousy is meditation. Just sit upright in a chair or lie down. After a few deep breaths, close your eyes. Focus on your breathing and, whenever you become distracted, bring your mind back to the breath. You'll probably spend a good portion of the session distracted, which is fine. You'll begin to notice how often those negative thoughts of jealousy come up, and you will become more aware of them in general.

It's more than understandable that those with chronic illness sometimes feel jealous of their friends who are healthier. But using the tips, affirmations, and exercises laid out here should take some of the edge off that envy.

Day 20

Getting in Touch with Your Inner Child

Recap

How did it go squashing jealousy yesterday? I know it can be difficult to do, but, once you do, you'll feel so much freer and ready to accomplish those goals in your life that will bring you immense joy without feeling upset about someone else's accomplishments. Now that you have released the jealousy monster, you probably feel happy, content, and full of hope and faith. These are very good emotions to have. One way to hold on to them and maximize their effectiveness is to get in touch with your inner child.

Living with chronic illness not only wears down the state of your body but also wears down your state of mind (not to mention your spirit). Just ask another warrior—it's extremely difficult to live day in and day out with so many obstacles and limitations in your way.

It is perfectly normal to become frustrated, impatient, or even depressed at how much your life has changed as a result of your condition. As much as I'm urging you to embrace positive change in your life, it would be foolish of me to ignore how frustrated we all get about how chronic illness can be overwhelming at times.

Sometimes this pressure builds and builds until you're ready to explode with negative moods or words. On the surface, these raw emotions may feel good initially but often bring out impulsive, impetuous behavior that you often feel guilty about afterward. After all, when you feel so miserable, sad, and neglected, it's hard to focus on others and cater to their needs. You're probably thinking of a specific outburst right now.

So the next time you reach your boiling point and feel as if you're ready to explode with negativity, **take a very deep breath (or two) and know that these feelings are more than pure anger.** Instead realize that your body, your mind, and your spirit are trying to get your attention.

Your inner child—that part of you before we became wrapped up in "being an adult"—is begging you to focus on yourself and your needs. Right now. Realize that it's time to give in to your inner child and pacify him or her with some much needed "me time" that will rejuvenate and replenish your mood and make you feel better.

Being an adult doesn't mean you have to push aside those feelings. Instead it means that you must acknowledge, accept, and take responsibility for your own happiness and not allow other people's needs to trump yours. By focusing on you, and learning to listen to your body and what it is telling you, **you will show your inner child that you are important and that you care about your own happiness**.

You will validate your inner child's feelings of denial, neglect, disparagement, abandonment, or rejection by acknowledging them as important. In turn, your inner child will step back and allow you to feel happier, less moody and guilty. You will regain your innocence, wonder, awe, joy, sensitivity, and playfulness from childhood while gaining a happy and carefree attitude, just like you were as a child.

By taking time to nourish your inner child and consciously communicating with that little girl or boy within (think of your old yearbook photo if that helps!), listening to how he or she feels and what he or she needs from you here and now, you will feel better emotionally and physically, and will be better equipped to handle your needs and other people's needs too.

By learning to take your inner child seriously and put his/her needs first, you gain control and are rewarded with more happiness and inner peace. By treating your inner child like any good parent who provides their child with discipline, limits, boundaries, structure, AND unconditional love, support, nurturance, and acceptance, you strengthen the bond between you two.

By initiating and maintaining an ongoing dialogue with your inner child, the mature adult can be reached. A new mutually beneficial, cooperative, symbiotic relationship can be created in which the sometimes-conflicting needs of both the adult self and the inner child can be creatively satisfied. Sound good? You bet it is.

Today's Activities:

Here are some activities to help you get in touch with your inner child:

1. Reserve thirty minutes two to three times a week for physical activity. Your inner child loves physical activity. Of course working within the limitations of your illness and with the go-ahead from your doctor, try to work a few thirty-minute blocks of exercise into your week, like walking, dancing, playing sports (ping-pong, tennis, swimming, etc.). At the very least, play some video or board games.

2. Reserve one hour each week for creative expression. Expressing your creativity through writing, painting, crafts, etc., will engage your inner child's expansive imagination.

3. Rewatch a favorite comedy film or tell a funny story. Nothing connects you with your playful inner child quite like laughter.

Today's Affirmation:

Repeating this **affirmation** in front of the mirror ten times each morning will help to nurture your inner child:

"The child in me and I are one. We love each other, care for each other, appreciate each other, and will always belong to each other."

Day 21

Rejuvenate Your Mind, Body, and Soul

Recap

Yesterday we talked a bit about making peace with your inner child. You now know that ignoring your inner child is a recipe for disaster. Not only will he/she demand attention, but your refusal to honor him/her will lead to sadness, frustration, and negativity. In essence, ignoring your inner child will lead to unhappiness.

Today we're going to spend time talking about the importance of rejuvenating your mind, body, and soul.

How You Can Nurture Yourself

Nurturing ourselves consistently is essential to everyone, but it becomes especially important when you suffer from a chronic illness. Life with a chronic illness is incredibly difficult and sometimes feels impossible. When you put everyone else's needs first, you feel drained, exhausted, and overwhelmed.

Just like it is important to nurture your inner child, you must also rejuvenate your mind, body, and spirit. When you don't, you feel even worse mentally and physically. Your body responds with more pain flare-ups, irritability, and stress. Your needs feel unmet, and your life feels off balance. You live in a state of constant stress and unrest. As you might imagine, this takes a huge toll on your mental and physical health. Your relationships with others suffer as well, since you may feel irritable, impatient, and resentful about all you do for others and the fact that you're not tending to your own needs.

Fortunately it does not have to stay that way. The most powerful way to transform the stress and overwhelm in your life is by nurturing yourself consistently. Not just one day but every single day. And, as the saying goes, some of the best health care is self-care. So it's time to take care of yourself.

Since we recognize that our minds, bodies, and souls are connected, it is important to find ways to nurture ourselves that feed all three. When we do, we elevate our experience to one of sacred self-care.

Here are some activities you can do to nurture your mind, body, and soul:

1. Meditate. Stay with me on this one! Research shows that meditation has incredible benefits for the mind, body, and soul. Recent studies have shown that meditation is as helpful for decreasing depression as medication and also lowers the stress response in the body. As we know, people have been nurturing their souls for thousands of years with meditation. As a bonus, when we regularly meditate, we become more self-aware and thus make healthier choices for ourselves.

Whether you are a seasoned meditator or just a beginner, include the following self-nurturing practice in your day: Pause and breathe in and out intentionally a few times. Bringing the soul of curiosity rather than judgment, check in with your body for any discomfort or tension you may feel. Return to your breath for a few cycles; then notice your thoughts. Without chasing after them, label them: planning, worrying, regretting, etc. Return to your breath for a few more cycles. Meditation allows you to connect intentionally with your mind, body, and soul.

2. Be Creative. Creativity connects and nourishes our minds, bodies, and souls in a joyful, easy way. Expressing our creativity is a wonderful self-nurturing practice. You can nurture yourself in infinite creative ways, including drawing, coloring, collaging, painting, decorating your home or office, gardening, writing, dancing, singing, and/or playing an instrument. You do not need to identify as an artist to nurture yourself with creativity. You only need to allow yourself to express your authentic truth and beauty!

3. Play. Having unstructured and unscheduled time to play is so important for our health. Whether you are playing board games, a sport, or on the floor with your children or your dog, allowing yourself time to play and be in the moment is essential for living with more peace and joy. So give yourself permission today to play and have fun!

Empower yourself with these nurturing practices. Try one each day and reflect on the difference it makes in your overall health and wellness.

Today's Affirmation:

Here is an **affirmation** you can repeat five times in the mirror each morning to help you on your journey toward rejuvenating your body, mind, and soul:

"I need time to take care of myself before I can effectively care for others."

Today's Activity:

List three things you will do today to rejuvenate your mind, body, and soul.

_____

_____

_____

Say No to Guilt!

Conclusion

Congratulations! You've finished the twenty-one-day challenge. You go, chronic illness warrior—you go! Think about where you were mentally three weeks ago. Think about how you feel right now. If you've really dedicated yourself to change—and I think you have, otherwise you wouldn't be reading this right now—then you are in a much better place.

I'm so incredibly proud of you, and I am amazed by your power, strength, and perseverance. You didn't give up, and instead went through the daily activities with zeal and tenacity. I'm personally amazed by your power, strength, and fortitude. You are a force to be reckoned with.

Every day you plow through insurmountable obstacles, and you push aside your frustrations and despair. You never lose sight of hope and faith. **You imagine a brighter future with better health, more peace, and more happiness, and you know it is in your grasp.**

Hopefully through this twenty-one-day journey together, you have found the inner peace and happiness that you deserve. You have sent guilt packing and learned to put your needs first, rediscovered how blessed you are, found new methods of stress reduction (like meditation or yoga), learned how to embrace your condition with unconditional love (as you work to improve your health), discovered new ways to handle setbacks, and more.

Like a rainbow is seen after a storm, I see a brighter future for you, despite your chronic illness storm.

That's what I want for you: to live a life you've always wanted *despite* chronic illness, rather than a life you never wanted *because* of chronic illness. The difference between *despite* and *because* is perseverance and effort, and you have both in spades.

If you ever lose your way, remember that you have the power to change your life. You have the power to say no to guilt and to say yes to inner peace and happiness. You have the power to change your life—one day at a time. You've got this!

Your fellow warrior,
Kristi

PS: Want to keep the conversation going? Connect with me on Twitter at @successthang or visit my website at http://www.successthang.com

Free VIP Readers Group Offer

Want a free report specifically for chronic illness warriors who desire unconditional love and acceptance? Kristi Patrice Carter is offering *Learning to Love Myself As I Am* for free (no strings attached). This amazing report is available to members of her VIP readers group. To download it, click hyperlink or visit https://www.instafreebie.com/free/nkteb

Other Books by Kristi Patrice Carter on Amazon

Say Yes to Success Despite Your Chronic Illness: 10 Weeks to Overcoming the Obstacles of Chronic Illness and Finally Achieving What You Want in Life

Passive Income Streams: How to Create and Profit from Passive Income Even If You're Cash-Strapped and a Little Bit Lazy (But Motivated)!

Wean that Kid: Your Comprehensive Guide to Understanding and Mastering the Weaning Process

I'm a Weaned Kid Now

Bonus

Happiness, Inner Peace, and Joy Affirmations and Other Great Resources

Affirmations for Chronic Illness Warriors Who Want to Say No to Guilt and Want to Achieve Happiness, Inner Peace, and Joy

1. Taking care of my needs is important to me and those around me. The people I love want me to be at my best, which means making my health a priority.
2. I feel proud of the steps I take to prioritize my health.
3. I can accomplish everything I need to accomplish. The rest can wait.
4. I am worthy of all good things—love, joy, peace, and abundance.
5. I am doing the best I can with what I have, and it is always enough.
6. I lovingly accept myself and all that I can accomplish today.
7. I love and accept myself as I am.
8. I gently hold my heart in my hands and protect myself from all negativity.
9. I release all negative thoughts and self-criticism. I am good enough today.
10. I lovingly accept myself right where I am today.
11. Peace, love, and joy are all that I allow into my thoughts today.
12. I am loved and cared for. I am enough.
13. I choose only healing positive thoughts today.
14. I will not allow my chronic illness to prevent me from pursuing all the happiness life has to offer.
15. I am worthy of all the best life has to offer.
16. I'm getting better every single day.
17. My body is working hard to improve its health.
18. I'm learning how to feel happier each moment.
19. I am stronger than this. I have the power to control my thoughts. My pain is a liar. I can handle this.
20. I will not dwell on the bad in life. Instead I will focus my energy on the good.
21. It is not my responsibility to shoulder the burdens of others. It is my responsibility to take care of myself. I will continue to

put my needs and happiness first.

22. I am on my own unique journey, and I will not compare myself to others.

23. I am not defined by my illness, and I won't let it hold me back from achieving my dreams.

24. I am happy for my friends' good health and do not envy them.

25. The child in me and I are one. We love each other, care for each other, appreciate each other, and will always belong to each other.

26. I need time to take care of myself before I can effectively care for others.

27. I am committed to loving myself right now. I am not perfect, but I am fantastic. I am a dynamic human being, and my life has purpose and meaning. I will love myself despite any imperfections. Those imperfections make me, me. I am grateful for everything my body does on a daily basis to keep me alive and uplifted. My body and I are working toward better health, and I will love myself unconditionally—starting today!

28. I'm a warrior. I am [insert your name], and I love myself very much.

29. Hi, [insert your name]. I'm willing to love you. [Best done as mirror work.]

30. Today I will set SMART goals for myself. They will be Specific, Measureable, Attainable, Relevant, and Timely. I will achieve every goal I set out to accomplish in due time. I will feel proud of my accomplishments today and every day.

31. I am amazing, and I must always put myself first. By planning for situations that I can't control, I stay committed to my goals and happiness.

32. I am not yet well, but I am getting better every day. In time, my health will improve.

33. I didn't cause my illness, and I shouldn't feel guilty about it. Guilt and shame will only win if I allow them to. I choose to be in control of any guilty feelings and to see the best in my life and my situation. I chose happiness now.

Happiness, Inner Peace and Joy Organizations

Global Happiness Organization

A nonprofit organization that focuses on the scientific basis of happiness. GHO's mission is to promote happiness and reduce suffering in the world.

+46 704 417188
S:t Petrigången 1, 211 22 Malmö, Sweden
Org no: 802433-8751
info@globalhappiness.com
us@globalhappiness.com

Free membership or paying member, US $4.00/month
http://www.globalhappiness.com/us

Global Peace through Happiness

578 A, Maha Laxmi Nagar,
Indore (M.P.)-452001 India
0731-2576324
0731-2576324
info@happinessforyou.org

Chief Executive Officer Vivek Singh, ceo@happinessforyou.org
Vivek Singh is passionate about his belief that happiness is simple and attainable by all. He says, "The ultimate aim of our life is to become happy. Happiness is a universal common goal."

www.happinessforyou.org

Pursuit of Happiness, Inc., 501(c)(3) EIN: 26–4756415

525 W. Rainbow Blvd
Salida, CO 81201

A membership-based group that offers monthly webinars and workshops on building happy communities.

$19.95/month. Student rate $10.00. First month free.
www.pursuit-of-happiness.org

Happiness Club

The mission of the Happiness Club is to share the benefits of being happy; utilizing resources, such as in-person meetings, newsletters, and a web presence.

Lionel Ketchian, PrintLRK@aol.com
Fairfield Happiness Club
63 Unquowa Road
Fairfield, CT 06824
(203) 258-7777

http://www.happinessclub.com

Authentic Happiness

A research-based site which shares scientific research on happiness and positive thinking. This group is run by University of Pennsylvania's Positive Psychology Center and Founder of Positive Psychology Martin Seligman.

https://www.authentichappiness.sas.upenn.edu

Delivering Happiness

Developed around the book written by Tony Hsieh, CEO of Zappos. Their mission is to promote happiness within corporate organizations and other work environments.

http://deliveringhappiness.com/

European Network for Positive Psychology

A European research-based site, sharing results of scientific studies on Positive Psychology.

http://www.enpp.eu/

Happify

Happify is an app that offers science-based games and activities to reduce negative thoughts and stress.

http://www.happify.com/

Happiness and Its Causes

An Australian-based site that shares tips and techniques to achieve happiness, as determined by data from science, philosophy, and religion.

http://www.happinessanditscauses.com.au/

Intentional Insights

Research into cognitive psychology and behavioral economics, this site has tools to help you set and reach goals.

http://intentionalinsights.org/

International Positive Psychology Association

Focused on the science of positive psychology, including increasing the research of positive psychology actions and results around the world.

http://www.ippanetwork.org/

Positive Psychology Center at the University of Pennsylvania

The hub for all research, training, and education, led by Martin Seligman, founder of the positive psychology movement.

http://www.positivepsychology.org/

Positive Psychology Network

A research-based network that promotes positive psychology for individual and group benefits.

http://www.positive-psychology-network.com/

Positive Psychology Program at Claremont Graduate University

One of only two colleges in the country to offer an MA and a PhD in Positive Psychology. Founded by Mihaly Csikszentmihalyi.

http://www.cgu.edu/positivepsych/

Happier with Gretchen Rubin

Founded by the author of the book *The Happiness Project*, Gretchen Rubin, this site shares stories and the science of happiness from around the world.

http://www.gretchenrubin.com/

The World Database of Happiness

This site tracks scientific research on happiness to share with the public.

http://worlddatabaseofhappiness.eur.nl/

Values in Action (VIA) Institute on Character

This site focuses on improving the character of individuals. The site offer a free survey to determine character strengths.

https://www.viacharacter.org/

Wholebeing Institute

An educational organization designed to promote the sharing of happiness practices in all areas of a person's life.

https://wholebeinginstitute.com/

Happiness, Inner Peace, and Joy Books

Happiness

Simple Reminders: Inspiration for Living Your Best Life by Bryant McGill and Jenni Young

This book shares concrete tips and activities to help individuals find happiness in their life. Beautiful artwork and photography are included throughout the book.

http://amzn.to/1FdGPeb

Being You, Changing the World by Dr. Dain Heer

Written by chiropractor Dain Heer, after a period of extreme depression. *Being You* details how to improve your life and become happy in practical, easy-to-implement ways.

http://amzn.to/1JnK6m2

Emergence: Seven Steps for Radical Life Change by Derek Rydall

Focuses on the ancient principles shared by life coach Derek Rydall, who believes and teaches to look within to find your purpose and achieve happiness.

http://amzn.to/1V8X8KW

The Happiness Project: Or Why I Spent a Year Trying to Sing in the Morning, Clean My Closets, Fight Right, Read Aristotle, and Generally Have More Fun by Gretchen Rubin

A yearlong look at science-based research, coupled with one woman's attempt to find happiness. She shares her experiences candidly in an effort to show you how to apply them to your life for greater joy.

http://amzn.to/1OtaeUk

Inner Peace

***Inner Peace: Stepping into Serenity to Find Peace of Mind* by Andy Lacroix**

Focusing on a three-step method called the Triple A Way, the book looks at barriers to inner peace and how to ultimately achieve peace in your life.

http://amzn.to/1FdHlss

***The Presence Process - A Journey into Present Moment Awareness* by Michael Brown**

This book teaches readers to exercise full personal responsibility with a practical approach to reaching personal peace, regardless of what's happening in the real world around us.

http://amzn.to/1KMgMe9

***Journey to Nowhere: A Spiritual Comedy* by Munish Markan**

A story told in the style of a fable about a student's path to spiritual enlightenment while encountering three friends along the journey.

http://amzn.to/1NKMZn4

Wherever You Go, There You Are by Jon Kabat-Zinn

The author is the founder of the Stress Reduction Clinic at the University of Massachusetts Medical Center and author of *Full Catastrophe Living*. His focus is on mindfulness—the act of living fully in the present moment while observing ourselves, our feelings, and our surroundings.

http://amzn.to/1V8ndPs

Joy

Living with Joy: Keys to Personal Power and Spiritual Transformation by Sanaya Roman

This book is filled with meditations and exercises to help the reader reach their highest potential, focusing on positivity and joy.

http://amzn.to/2bdF1G1

Fight Back with Joy: Celebrate More. Regret Less. Stare Down Your Greatest Fears by Margaret Feinberg

Written by a cancer survivor based on her own experience with choosing joy to live her life and battle her illness.

http://amzn.to/1NRMQjj

Simple Abundance: A Daybook of Comfort of Joy by Sarah Ban Breathnach

An essay compilation designed for women who wish to live joyfully by following their authentic selves and finding joy in the everyday activities and rhythm of life.

http://amzn.to/1gKRQaJ

Happiness, Inner Peace, and Joy Documentaries

The Peace Experience

The story of one group's journey through various countries to find and share inner peace.

http://imdb.to/1V8ZVDM

How to Live Forever: Results May Vary

A look at what it's like to grow old and how living forever might appear. This documentary includes interviews with the elderly, and the habits and daily lifestyles that they believe have kept them living a long life.

http://www.liveforevermovie.com

Life in a Day

A look at how all of us, regardless of our culture or background, struggle with the same fears and anxieties.

http://amzn.to/2bepZ6d

I Am

A look at an accident victim who had a near-death experience and how positive thinking has transformed his life and helped him heal.

http://amzn.to/1MHjTGB

Happy

A scientific study on the cause of happiness, featuring interviews with people from various cultures and backgrounds.

http://amzn.to/1Ote3Jg

A Joyful Mind

A beginner's look at meditation and how it can help others, focusing on the sense of peace and well-being it offers in chaotic times.

http://www.ajoyfulmind.com

Living Luminaries: On the Serious Business of Happiness

Interviews with some of the world's most renowned inspirational leaders of our time, including Eckhart Tolle, Marianne Williamson, and Don Miguel Ruiz, as well as many others.

http://www.livingluminaries.com/

https://www.facebook.com/llfilm#sthash.JaePtirj.dpuf

Euphoria

A look at the pursuit of happiness in America and answering the question, "Is it working?"

http://amzn.to/1Kz3YV7

Happiness Is an Inside Job

A look at finding deeper contentment as opposed to finding happiness based on circumstances and surroundings.

http://amzn.to/1G1aoKN

About the Author

Kristi Patrice Carter is a wife, mother, author, businesswoman, and chronic illness warrior. Although she suffers from fibromyalgia and chronic pain, she hasn't allowed either to diminish her creativity, compassion, or desire to help chronic illness warriors live truly radiant lives.

A force to be reckoned with, Carter earned a Bachelor of Arts in English from the University of Illinois and a Juris Doctorate from Chicago-Kent College of Law, and has over seventeen years of experience in the writing industry. She is the author of:

- *Say Yes to Success Despite Your Chronic Illness: 10 Weeks to Overcoming the Obstacles of Chronic Illness and Finally Achieving What You Want in Life!*

- *Wean That Kid: Your Comprehensive Guide to Understanding and Mastering the Weaning Process*

- *I'm a Weaned Kid Now*

- *Passive Income Streams: How to Create and Profit from Passive Income Even If You're Cash-Strapped and a Little Bit Lazy (But Motivated)!*

Carter is also the founder of http://www.successthang.com, where she helps other warriors find life outside of chronic pain through her empathy, passion, and love for life and people.

hanks for your purchase. You are twenty-one days away from chieving inner peace and happiness. Please download our free ompanion guide, at https://www.instafreebie.com/free/bw0yY. The assword is AlwaysGuiltFree. This comprehensive journal will enable ou to fully participate in the daily activities for maximum benefits.

Made in the USA
Columbia, SC
13 June 2017